THE G.O.A.T EFFECT
DEXAUS EVERSONS

AF430616

Copyright © Dexaus Eversons

All Rights Reserved.

Table of Contents

Foreword

This book has been self-published with all reasonable efforts taken to make the material error-free by the author. No part of this book shall be used, reproduced in any manner whatsoever without written permission from the author, except in the case of brief quotations embodied in critical articles and reviews.

The Author of this book is solely responsible and liable for its content including but not limited to the views, representations, descriptions, statements, information, opinions and references ["Content"]. The Content of this book shall not constitute or be construed or deemed to reflect the opinion or expression of the Publisher or Editor. Neither the Publisher nor Editor endorse or approve the Content of this book or guarantee the reliability, accuracy or completeness of the Content published herein and do not make any representations or warranties of any kind, express or implied, including but not limited to the implied warranties of merchantability, fitness for a particular purpose. The Publisher and Editor shall not be liable whatsoever for any errors, omissions, whether such errors or omissions result from negligence, accident, or any other cause or claims for loss or damages of any kind, including without limitation, indirect or consequential loss or damage arising out of use, inability to use, or about the reliability, accuracy or sufficiency of the information contained in this book.

I

How to be the G.O.A.T.(Greatest of All Time)

It is the dream of many but is attained by few when they talk about the title of the G.O.A.T, or Greatest of All Time. Be it an athlete, entrepreneur, artist, or in any other profession, becoming the best in the world requires a cocktail of mindset, discipline, strategy, and ceaseless hard work. This article breaks down the main principles and strategies needed to reach that coveted G.O.A.T level.

1. Adopt G.O.A.T. Mind-Set

-Believe in Yourself: Self-belief is the basis of becoming great. Doubts come in from all directions and from within oneself regarding achieving greatness. Acquire a faith in oneself that never turns.

- Cultivate a Growth Mindset: Being the G.O.A.T. is all about learning how to develop and grow on a day-to-day basis. Failures and setbacks are just one of the ways to improve. In fact, they are not failures themselves. You need to challenge yourself by continuous developing because you need to step out of your comfort zones.

- SET BOLD GOALS. If you want to be super great at something, then aim big. Your goals should push you out of your comfort zone. Break these big goals into actionable steps for a clear path forward.

3. Master Your Craft

Put in the Hours: Mastery is achieved only through deliberate practice. To be the G.O.A.T, one must put in far more time and effort than his competitor. It's not about coming back every day, even on days when you don't feel like it.

- Seek Constant Improvement: Analyze your performance regularly to identify areas for growth. This means embracing feedback, refining your techniques, and staying updated with the latest trends and innovations in your field.

- Study the Best: Observe and learn from those who are already at the top. Understand their methods, habits, and the paths they took to reach their level of excellence. Use their successes and failures as a roadmap to carve your own path.

3. Build Unbreakable Discipline

- Consistency Over Motivation: Motivation is a fleeting emotion, but discipline will push you to move closer to your goals day-in and day-out. You formulate a set of habits and routines that are geared toward aligning with the vision of becoming great. That means practice, proper nutrition, rest, and all other kinds of mental conditioning.

- Eliminate Distractions: Being a G.O.A.T means the elimination of everything that is not contributing toward your vision. Social media, harmful practices, and pointless activities create obstacles in achieving your goal. Find it in yourself to focus deeper on what you need to achieve.

- Mastering Time Management: Time is your most valuable resource. You can learn to concentrate on the things that will take you closer to what you want. Make use of productivity and efficiency time-block tools and the Pomodoro technique.

4. Build Mental Resilience:

- Embrace Failure as Part of the Process: Every G.O.A.T. has had their share of failure—sometimes even more than once. What makes one different is the ability to come back stronger from those setbacks in life. Make each setback a learning opportunity and keep moving on.

- Mindfulness and Meditation Practice: A peaceful mind is essential for peak performance. Such practices as meditation can help improve one's focus, reduce more stress, and clear the mind. Suggest visualization techniques to prepare for high-pressure situations.

- Achieve a Winning Mind-Set: Concentrate on your own performance and forget about what is happening in the competitors' realm. Turn adversities into opportunities that you can use to demonstrate your qualities. Develop a mental exercise that you can do when you're feeling doubtful or when problems seem insurmountable, such as positive affirmations or deep breathing.

5. Surround Yourself with Greatness:

Find a Mentor- A mentor can guide you, give you a viewpoint, and provide support all along the way. Look for someone who has walked down a similar path and can give you insight and encouragement.

Build a strong support network- No man or woman is an island, and great things cannot be achieved in isolation. Find folks who believe in your vision, challenge you to be better, and keep you accountable.

- Healthy Competition: You should ignore other people's journeys, but competition serves as a benchmark for growth. Seek your rivals who challenge you to strive to do better.

6. Master the Art of Adaptability:

- Stay Ahead of the Curve: And to be a G.O.A.T, you must be responsive and adaptable. Learn about the industry trends and technological progress and get aware of the new techniques and advancements. Those people who can quickly adapt to change easily turn challenges into opportunities.

Innovate and reinvent yourself: the best never settle with status quo. Constantly come up with new ways to improve, innovate, and make your craft stay fresh. This keeps you relevant and sets rather than follows trends.

Take the criticism and learn from it: There's good criticism and bad criticism. The constructive type of criticism serves as a tool to improve. Learn the difference between useful feedback and mere negativity. Use information gleaned from trusted sources and apply it to develop your craft.

7. Take care of your body and mind

- Prioritize physical fitness Physical fitness is pretty cut and dry: whether you are an athlete or not, it impacts your performance. Developing your physical fitness through regular exercise gives you endurance, energy, and concentration, so you can persevere over longer periods of effort.

Sleep like a champion: This is a physiological activity in which the body and mind recover. To keep yourself on top, you must need to rest for 7-9 hours of quality sleep, which enhances cognitive function, mood, and physical well-being.

- Fuel Your Body Right: Nutrition plays a huge role in energy levels and focus. Eat well by getting a balanced diet rich in proteins, healthy fats, and complex carbohydrates. Drinking plenty of water is also fundamental to maintaining high performance.

8. Give Back to Your Community

Mentor Others: Share your knowledge and experiences. This process helps others, but in return, it cements the gains that you make. It can even keep you humble and remind you of the journey you took to be where you are today.

- Do Greater Good: The G.O.A.T. does not define themselves by what is achieved but much more so by what community they touch. Do good as well by using what you have in life to better others positively in this world.

- Humility: Greatness is not about being number one, but about lifting people up with you. Keeping an attitude of humility will attract much more respect and keep your eyes open to continuous growth.

9. Legacy Goals:

- Be Better Than Yourself for the Long Haul: G.O.A.T. is not about achieving one great season or accomplishing one great project. Rather, it's about having sustainably high levels of excellence over time. Consider how you want to impact your field.

Create a vision of your legacy. How do you want to be remembered? Define what values and principles you want to contribute to. That in itself will give meaning to the journey you are on and will trigger you at difficult times.

Achieve Impact Rather than Recognition: Work towards impact rather than recognition. Provided your work adds value and makes a difference, recognition will follow.

10. Celebrate the Small Wins:

Recognize Progress: To become the G.O.A.T, we are into a long marathon. Thus, recognizing the progress helps boost one's morale and provides motivation to go on.

Reflect on How Far You Have Gone: Take a moment to reflect and evaluate the journey undertaken. Celebrate improvements, lessons learned, and steps completed. This reminded the person of how much they had grown and how much motivation they had received in order to be continued.

- Stay Hungry for More: Even after you are crowned as the top, continue working towards improvement. For the G.O.A.T., the journey never really ends. There is always another challenge to face, a new goal to reach, and a new level of mastery to attain.

Becoming the Best-Ending:

Becoming the G.O.A.T. is not a destination; it's a way of life. It means relentless pursuit, unwavering belief in your capacity, and being resolute in keeping moving forward. By mastering your craft, embracing discipline, and maintaining a growth mindset, you are bound to take over the top spots in your domain. Greatness is one step at a time. Begin today and have fun along the ride.

II
Famous G.O.A.T.s and What Made Them Great: A Case Study

An intriguing aspect of the concept of G.O.A.T.s is that this cuts across professions and industries, and individuals who attain this status have commonalities in the traits they exhibit that may include extraordinary commitment, resilience, and relentless pursuit of excellence.

In this case study, we look at several widely known G.O.A.T.s through different fields, their paths to greatness, and lessons from their journeys.

1. Michael Jordan (Basketball):

Achievements:

6 NBA Championships with the Chicago Bulls

5-time NBA MVP

14-time NBA All-Star

Inducted into the Basketball Hall of Fame

What Made Him Great:

- Unyielding Work Ethic: No one was better than Michael Jordan at being an improvement machine. Everyone knows that he woke up before the sun was up to practice and then spent so many additional hours developing that shot after he became a basketball superstar.

Resilience in Adversity: Jordan was cut from his basketball team in high school. That could have sent him down. However, it instead spurred him to prove himself. He energized with every failure, converting each down into a step up.

The competitiveness of Jordan-the measure by which all others are measured-he was made of the stuff of legends. His competitive ability never ceased to find a way to be pushed; in fact, he pushed his teammates in practice. His mind-set was, "I play to win, whether it's practice or a real game."

- Takeaway: Road to being G.O.A.T is one of constant pursuit and the courage to bounce back from failure. A fiery competitive spirit may be the difference between you and the rest.

2. Serena Williams (Tennis):

- Achievements:

23 Grand Slam singles titles (most of the Open Era)

- 4 Olympic gold medals

- Dominated tennis for more than two decades

- The pioneering African American female athlete in a sport with few such athletes at the top

- Why Great:

-Unequalled Discipline: A strong emphasis on training and constant preparation had allowed Serena Williams to maintain her peak performance even up to the late 30s. The extreme physical fitness regime and a strict diet therefore became key to her extended stay at the top.

- Mental Toughness: Serena has also been good at staying calm and focused while playing on match point when she is on the verge of losing. She has said several times that she visualized success and practiced mindfulness to keep herself calm during crucial moments.

- Advocacy and Resilience: Serena had to bear many attacks, including racist remarks and derogatory criticism of her physique and playing style. Never would she let such external ramifications deflect the path ahead. On the contrary, she used all that available machinery to lobby for equality in sports for women and to draw inspiration from all young athletes.

- Key Takeaway: Mental toughness and perseverance to get things done can be combined with disciplined prep work to ensure long-term success. Staying true to your values can, too, help to create an indelible mark beyond mere personal accomplishments.

3. Steve Jobs (Technology):

- Achievements:

Founded Apple Inc. and revolutionized the way several industries operate, mainly computers, smartphones, and digital music.

Led the creation of iconic products: iPhone, iPad, and MacBook Made Apple the most valuable company in the world

What Makes Him Great:

Visionary thinking: Jobs excelled in envisioning products that people didn't even know they needed. He concentrated on design and usability, hence the simplicity of technology products.

- Resilience in the Face of Failure: After being removed from Apple in 1985, Jobs could have thrown in the towel. Instead, he went on to found NeXT, as well as purchase Pixar, which would become incredibly successful in its own right. A return to Apple led to a string of groundbreaking products for the company.

Perfectionism and High Standards: Jobs was always demanding perfection from himself as well as from others on his team. He would involve himself in every detail of product development ensuring that whatever Apple designed met his lofty standards.

Key Takeaway: Greatness often depends on the clear vision of the future and the persistence with which one clings to it despite failure. Unyielding dedication to quality can make all the difference in any field.

4. Muhammad Ali (Boxing):

- Achievements:

- 3x World Heavyweight Champion

- Olympic Gold Medalist (1960)

He is famous for his epic battles with Joe Frazier, George Foreman, and others

What Made Him Great:

- Unique Style and Confidence: The style at which he boxed was revolutionary-high speed, footwork, and defensive technique. He said, "Float like a butterfly, sting like a bee," which would be the mantra of his unique approach to boxing.

- Boldness and Activism: Ali's greatness went far beyond the ring. He declined to be drafted into the Vietnam War, giving years of his career over principle. His actions in standing for what he believed are part of his iconic status in civil rights as much as they are in sports.

- Mental Strength: Ali used to enter his opponents' minds before the match. He believed in the strength of words, where he could use self-boosting words against himself and against his competitors.

- Takeaway: To be G.O.A.T. is to have both mastery over your craft and the use of your platform to stand for something. This confidence over your skills and boldness to take that step can take one's legacy further.

5. Oprah Winfrey (Media and Philanthropy)

-Accomplishments:

Host of The Oprah Winfrey Show, the most-viewed talk show in television history

- First African American billionaire

- Founder of OWN (Oprah Winfrey Network) and a powerful advocate for various social issues

- What Made Her Great:

- Empathy and Connection: The secret to Oprah's phenomenal success on the show lay in her ability to connect with the audience at a very visceral, emotional level. She listened and told their stories on her platform; this resonated with millions of people.

- Travails of Overcoming Adversity: Oprah's life has never been one of simplicity and comfort. Poverty and trauma define the early years of this great leader, yet she didn't let it mark her in any way; instead, she used this to give her the vigor to work hard and inspire many through this story.

- Diversification and Reinvention: Oprah didn't stop at television. She entered into publishing (O Magazine), produced movies, and started her own network. Such dynamism has served to keep her relevant for decades.

What truly lasting impact is made by the best. Real empathy to understand others, the ability to bring people together and to be one in an adverse situation wherein one remains resilient can at times make a difference. Continual reinvention makes the leader remain relevant.

6. Tom Brady (American Football)

- Awards:

- 7-time Super Bowl champion (most by any player)

- 5-time Super Bowl MVP

- Considers one of the greatest quarterbacks in NFL history

What Made Him Great:

-Unmatched Work Ethic: Drafted as the 199th pick, Brady was one dedicated man who 'converted' himself into perhaps the most successful quarterback in the sport, continually working to hone and build his skills and in-game acumen year upon year.

- Longevity and Adaptability: Brady's longevity in performing at the top level even until his 40s is as a result of keen interest and care towards diet, physical therapy, and living disciplined. His ability to adapt himself to the new system and teammates led him to success even when joining a different team, (Tampa Bay Buccaneers).

- Leadership: Brady raises those around him. Leadership on and off the field motivated and inspired teammates to push beyond their limits, creating that winning culture.

-Key Takeaway: Greatness comes from nothing but relentless effort toward improvement, adaptability in change, and an ability to inspire and elevate others.

Each of these G.O.A.T.s - belonging to a field as diverse as it gets - shares the same qualities that elevated them to the top:

Unwavering pursuit for betterment and excellence

The ability to emerge unbroken from setbacks, criticism

An approach or angle that was unique in some way, resonating with others

The ability to be a catalyst for action in other people

Their journeys show that being termed the G.O.A.T. is not because of talent but the mindset, habits, and values that drive them to succeed and help them reach heights others only dream of, so emulating those principles will help somebody striving to be great in life and career.

1. "The only person you are destined to become is the person you decide to be." — Ralph Waldo Emerson

III

"12 Must-Read Books to Unlock the G.O.A.T. Within You"

Becoming the Greatest of All Time (G.O.A.T.) in your field means as much to do with mental fitness and not merely skills and knowledge. The right books can inspire you, arm you with a successful framework for greatness, or strategic action steps to nurture whatever quality greatness requires. Here is a list of the best books to help you develop the mindset, discipline, and resilience needed to bring out the G.O.A.T. inside you:

1. "Relentless: From Good to Great to Unstoppable" by Tim S. Grover

- Why It Matters: Written by the legendary coach of Michael Jordan, Kobe Bryant, and Dwyane Wade, among others, this book looks at what separates top performers from everyone else. Grover describes a mindset-the "Cleaner," so to speak-that achieves at the highest level, overcomes obstacles, and never settles for anything less than excellence.

- Key Takeaway: To become unstoppable, embrace the pressure, learn to own your flaws, and focus relentlessly on your goals.

2. "Mindset: The New Psychology of Success" by Carol S. Dweck

Why You Need to Read It: Dweck on the *growth mindset* is a must-read for anybody who wants to achieve greatness. She expounds on how the perception that the ability can be developed through effort and learning *growth mindset* is different from the limited outlook of people who believe that talents are innate fixed mindset.

The ability to perceive challenges as opportunities for improvement will be a key takeaway from having a growth mindset-this is one of the main reasons people will be G.O.A.T.

3. "Can't Hurt Me: Master Your Mind and Defy the Odds" by David Goggins

Why Is It Important?

David Goggins- human manifestation of the endless limits to which we can push the human endurance level. It begins with standing extreme physical tests through the experience of being a Navy SEAL to now ultra-endurance athlete, sharing his approach of "calloused mind" in the removal of barriers.

The book will help you discover the inner strength inside you, break down those mental barriers to transform pains into powers, and build up the necessary resilience to achieve greatness.

4. "Atomic Habits: An Easy & Proven Way to Build Good Habits & Break Bad Ones" James Clear

- Why It Matters: Good things come from doing small things repeatedly. What James Clear suggests offers practical frameworks for forming habits that stick and eliminating those that hinder you from getting closer to your best.

Key Takeaway: Improvement is 1% better than before. Compounding small habits to create massive success makes it possible to be the G.O.A.T. in your space.

5. "The Obstacle Is the Way: The Timeless Art of Turning Trials into Triumph" by Ryan Holiday

-Why It's a Must Read: Combining Stoic thoughts, Holiday recounts how the adoption of challenges and obstacles as opportunities can be a pathway to success in the long run. This kind of thought can be used to build up mental willpower that would allow individuals to bear setbacks with dignity.

- Takeaway: Distress can become a way forward, and failure often becomes a stepping stone to success.

6. "Grit: The Power of Passion and Perseverance" by Angela Duckworth

-Why It's A must-read: Angela Duckworth's work establishes the idea of grit being passion and perseverance to keep going toward long-term goals as one of the greatest predictors for success, explaining in the book how tenacity and resilience are more important than raw talent.

Takeaway

Status of G.O.A.T.-To become the status of G.O.A.T., it is going to require you to go through the grind and dedicate yourself to your goal. You will be very patient and tolerant with your journeys as things are going slow.

7. "The 10X Rule: The Only Difference Between Success and Failure"byGrantCardone

Key Take-A-Ways -

Why It's Important: This book by Grant Cardone shows us his philosophy of massive action gets extraordinary results. He reminds us often that most people have no clue how much effort is actually required in order to attain the big goal. It often creates 10 times more value than you would originally think of getting.

KEY TAKEAWAY To be called G.O.A.T, one has to be operating way above the ordinary "normal" effort. He or she must take bold actions toward his or her vision.

8. "The Champion's Mind: How Great Athletes Think, Train, and Thrive" by Jim Afremow

- Why It's Important: Authored by a sports psychologist, this book offers practical strategies for becoming a champion. The prescriptions include mental training, goal setting, and visualization techniques used by elite athletes.

Key Takeaway: The champion mindset is actually about being in the right mental preparation, with the ability to stay not only focused but composed under pressure-things that those who wish to be at the top of their game should be aware of.

9. "Start with Why: How Great Leaders Inspire Everyone to Take Action" by Simon Sinek

- Why It Matters: This is a book on leadership, but really, its principles are more applicable for those aspiring to greatness. To Sinek, "knowing your why" - or having a deep reason for doing something - drives great success and inspires others.

- Key Takeaway: Knowing your "why" brings you the motivation to push forward against obstacles and lets you not lose your focus on your highest goals.

10. "Outliers: The Story of Success" by Malcolm Gladwell:

- Why You'll Like It: Gladwell digs behind the scenes and finds what makes great successes different, such as the "10,000-hour rule," which points out that it takes around 10,000 hours of deliberate practice to be mastered.

Bottom Line Key Takeaway: The ends can make the means, but consistent effort with timely and proper opportunities surely overshadows the rest. Understanding this context of success will help you map your own path to greatness.

11. "The Art of War" by Sun Tzu:

- Why It Matters: This old book gives timeless strategic insight applicable to today's business, sports, or personal development challenges. It teaches preparation and adaptability.

- The takeaway is that one needs to become able to think strategically if he wants to be a G.O.A.T. - in other words, someone who can adapt to any changing circumstances and outmaneuver his opponents, qualities which Sun Tzu's philosophies place at the core of such success.

12. High Performance Habits: How Extraordinary People Become That Way by Brendon Burchard

- Why It's Essential: Burchard looks into what separates high performers from the crowd-life focus, productivity, and influence, among other habits-and shares actionable advice on how to create such habits in your own life.

Conclusion - High performance does not happen by accident-it results from habits developed through focused effort and self-discipline.

Books to Fuel Your Journey of Greatness:

Each of these books provides distinctive insights into the qualities, habits, and mindsets that define the G.O.A.T. of any field. They do not only inspire but they give you actionable strategies that you can apply to your journey. Reading these books can therefore help you digest the discipline, resilience, and vision it would take for you to reach the top of your game. Whether in athletics, business success, or mastery in any craft, these books will serve as guides on how to unlock that G.O.A.T within you.

IV
Mental Exercises for Optimum Fitness Levels

There are plenty of physical exercises and their benefits documented accurately across the world. There are several benefits of exercising daily right from keeping your blood pressure in check to keeping heart diseases and other problems at bay. It has also been noted that physical exercises keep the physical appearance also bright and neat. With time, the benefits of physical exercises have been focused on the mental health and state, i.e. several exercises lift mood and improve sleep by reducing stress and anxiety. Along with a healthy heart and functioning joints, keeping your mind calm and focusing on your emotional wellbeing is also essential.

In this blog, we will be talking about exercises that are centered around the mind and mental health so that by focusing on them you can reach the optimum fitness level and become a high performer. The phrase 'use it or lose it' applies to the brain functioning very effortlessly.

What is brain training?

Brain training includes mental exercises which focus on the mind and functioning of the brain. In addition to that, mental exercises if performed correctly have also boosted intelligence and emotional wellbeing among people. There are several brain exercises that you could perform from time to time to keep your brain sharp and working efficiently.

Mental or brain exercises to keep your fitness at an optimum level

We are mentioning below some of the most effective yet easy brain and mental exercises which you could take up so that you can focus better on work and remain calm. The below exercises are very common among people and can be performed by the majority of people irrespective of age. Right from jigsaw puzzles to taking a stroll in the garden, you could perform these activities easily.

Solving jigsaw puzzles

Regardless of how big your jigsaw puzzle is, it strengthens your brain. It creates several cognitive abilities and prevents visuospatial cognitive aging. It challenges the brain and makes it work till you can fit the missing pieces of the puzzles.

Card games

If you don't remember the last time you played cards, then it is time for you to shuffle those decks of cards. Playing card games increases the brain volume in several brain regions and also increases memory and thinking skills. You could give solitaire, hearts, poker, crazy eights, and even rummy a shot. Card games not only sharpen your cognitive skills but also enhance your retention power.

Building up your vocabulary

One of the best ways to become smart and enhance your brain functions is through improvising on your vocabulary. Quick vocabulary sessions can get converted into brain stimulation sessions very easily. All you have to do is keep a notebook and go through different new words. Look up their meanings on the internet or in the dictionary and try using that word in your daily conversations. Vocabulary building is known to boost auditory and visual processing.

Learning a new skill

To strengthen the connections of your brain, you could take up a new skill. New skills are not only fun and interesting to learn and develop but also keep our brains hot and running. Studies have shown that new skill development contributes to the enhancement of memory function in the brain. You could take up new skills to not only kill time but also help your brain function strengthen.

Listening to music and dancing your heart out

Studies have shown that listening to music not only boosts mood but also enhances brain potential and creative thinking of the same. It is one of the easiest ways to enhance your brainpower. You can also take up learning new instruments and develop not only your skills but also increase your memory power.

In addition to that, dancing improves the memory and speed of the brain. You could take up dance classes of any form. It could not only help you in developing a skill but also allow you to have a better mood and brain functioning.

Meditation

Taking time out to meditate not only calms your body but also slows your breathing and brings peace to your mind. It has been seen that taking time out to meditate regularly makes your brain work smoothly and calmly. It fine-tunes the memory and also increases brain stability. All you have to do is find a quiet spot, sit down properly, close your eyes, and then spend time introspecting or just putting attention on one spot.

Now that you are aware of the mental exercises which will help your body to relax, you will be able to reach your fitness goal with ease. Focus on keeping your brain alert, memory retained and mind strengthened and calmed so that you can focus on the other factors that will ensure that your body is reaching the optimum fitness levels.

"Believe you can, and you're halfway there." — Theodore Roosevelt

V
Positive Affirmations To Change Your Life

To become successful, positive affirmations are extremely important. If the positive affirmations are done consistently and properly, they can prevent the human mind from thinking negatively. Positive affirmations can help you in remodelling your mind and eliminate the limiting beliefs.

Success is a mind game. If you think about yourself as a person who can achieve anything when having a focus on it, then the chances are high that you might end up achieving it. Positive affirmations are communication between the conscious and subconscious parts of the mind. Positive affirmations appear to be unfamiliar, but we use them every day without thinking about them.

The value of positive affirmations

The one and the only reason why many people don't reach their potential is due to their failure in taking action to reach their goals and dreams. They continue to believe the limiting factors their parents or friends have given to them. For achieving your goal in life, you need to have the courage to keep moving forward. Moreover, it becomes vital for anyone to speak positive affirmations for success every day.

Because when you speak a positive affirmation for success, it sends a positive message to the subconscious mind. Thus an excellent positive affirmation can help you in creating wealth, good health, and social status in life.

Positive affirmations which you should speak about every day.

Speaking positive affirmations can provide you the correct attitude for achieving success even under challenging circumstances.

My body is fit, my mind is productive, and my soul is calm.

The characteristic of a healthy body is a healthy mind and soul. If any of the three parameters suffers from negative emotions, the others will also be affected. The main reason behind the person's poor health is the individual itself. A human mind has the capability to remove every permission that they have subconsciously or consciously given to all the wrong things in the world.

By speaking this affirmation every day, you are going to defeat your negative mindset and come on top.

I believe I can do anything

Some people start thinking they will drown before even jumping into the deep ocean. However, this is the wrong way of tackling situations because once you say, "I can't do this," a barrier is created in mind. Your brain starts taking the negative approach of finding flaws in the objective.

The correct method to counter any challenge in life is to say, "I believe I can do anything," because once you say these words, the chances are high that you will succeed in doing it because your brain will start thinking about different ways which can be used to complete the task.

Everything which is happening now is happening for my good

When something wrong happens with them, many people start thinking that why only bad happens with them? They start doubting their self-worth based on an incident that has given them sadness. Feeling setback after a loss is natural, but pondering about it and thinking about how helpless you are is wrong.

Instead, people who have been through a setback about which they can't do anything shouldn't ponder upon it and derive negative results. Instead, they should think that "whatever has happened has happened for good." When they feel this way, positive energy is generated in the brain, which gives them the power for overcoming sadness and becoming productive.

I am the architect of my own life; I have chosen the foundation and will also select the contents.

Positive affirmations for becoming successful are things that you tell your brain when you wake up in the morning. Every new day is a new beginning and brings new challenges that might impact you and the people around you. Thus beginning your day with a positive affirmation will help you feel more productive and motivated towards achieving your goal.

Moreover, the above-mentioned affirmation will also give you the courage to take calculative risks in life without thinking about the consequences. Thus taking a risk will help you find the right and the wrongs about a particular approach. Therefore, it is highly essential that you carry a positive mind-set throughout the day.

I forgive anyone who have harmed me in the past and peacefully move away from them.

Getting hurt by someone is a part of life, and it should be considered a normal human trait. However, sometimes people get hurt. They find it extremely difficult to tackle the situation because of the emotions involved in the process. Then they start developing a hatred for the person who has hurt them, which is the beginning of creating a negative mind-set.

A person who develops a hatred for others is constantly feeding negative thoughts in their mind, which is dangerous for mental peace. Instead, they should forgive the person and create their own limits so that their mental stability is intact and the relation is held on.

Meta Description- If the positive affirmations are followed consistently and properly, they can prevent the human mind from thinking negatively

"Success is not the key to happiness. Happiness is the key to success." — Albert Schweitzer

VI
5 Tips to Improve the Quality of Your Sleep

Sleep is essential for our body to recover and repair. It is also a way to rejuvenate ourselves and face a new day. Studies conducted on the brain that is sleep deprived or gets less sleep shows that poor sleeping patterns have direct adverse effects on our normal brain functioning, everyday performance, and hormones. Lack of sleep causes us to gain weight, increasing the risk of obesity and diabetes in children and adults alike. It is also linked to poor mental and physical performance. Nowadays, because of longer working times and shorter nights, people are more prone to getting lesser and lesser sleep. This disrupts our regular sleep pattern, hence making it very difficult for our body to refresh and make new cells and store new information. Getting a good night's sleep is crucial if you want to optimize your overall health.

Here are some tips that will help you to sleep better at night.

Increase light exposure during the day.

The more light you are exposed to, the more your body will keep you awake. Light affects your mind, body, and hormones, helping you stay awake and be productive. Your body has its own natural timekeeping clock. This is called the circadian rhythm, and it tells you when to stay up and when to sleep. Letting in natural sunlight or any other source of bright light throughout the day keeps your circadian rhythm in check. It gives you the energy needed to pull through the day, as well as wind down for rest during the night. Natural sunlight is preferred over artificial light, but if you are unable to attain sunlight then artificial lights will help keep your circadian rhythm healthy and in check. This helps if you're an insomniac, as studies show that when an insomniac person was exposed to sunlight for a certain duration every day, their bodies gradually adjusted to the natural day and night pattern, helping them fall asleep.

Reduce Light Exposure in the Evening

Gradually as the day weans towards night, limit your exposure to bright light. At night, your body doesn't require much energy since you will be completely at rest. Exposing your body to lights, especially blue lights, will mess up your circadian rhythm, making you stay awake since your body thinks it is daytime. The consequences of this are that your brain reduces the secretion of melatonin, a hormone responsible for sleep and relaxation. Blue lights are found vastly in electronic gadgets such as smartphones and computers. People are more at risk of staying awake or having disruptive sleep patterns when they handle their phones or computers too much since these devices emit large amounts of blue light. There are several ways and apps to counter this.

• Wear orange tinted glasses or glasses that specifically block out blue light.

• Download apps such as f.lux or twilight to block out blue light on your phone and computer.

• Do not watch any electronic screen, whether it be your TV, laptop or phone, 2 hours prior to bed.

Avoid caffeine late into the day.

Caffeine is great if you want to keep up your energy levels and increase your attention span. There are many health benefits in relation to having caffeine. It is also the most widely consumed additive in most countries. Most people do not start their day without their cup of regular coffee and continue spilling caffeine into their system in the form of energy drinks and energy shots. A single dose of caffeine enhances our focus, gives us energy and drive.

However, when consumed later on, at the end of the day, caffeine overstimulates your nervous system, preventing you from winding down at night. Research shows that caffeine can stay in your bloodstream for up to 6 to 8 hours, hence having it before going to bed guarantees little to no sleep. You should stop your caffeine consumption before 1 p.m. if you want optimal night sleep and rest. And if you just cannot do without your regular daily coffee, then try the decaffeinated kind, which is gentler on your body, and is not as effective as regular coffee.

Reduce or avoid Long Daytime Naps.

For some people, getting their afternoon sleep is an important routine. There are studies that prove that short daytime naps, also called power naps, are highly beneficial. Taking a short nap can significantly reboot your brain power, increase memory and recollecting power, and gives you the capacity to store new information. The optimal time limit for a daytime nap can be a minimum of 15 minutes to a maximum of 1 hour. Anything more than that can negatively affect your sleep cycle.

Sleeping for long hours in the daytime can confuse your internal sleep clock, and in turn, you may struggle to fall asleep at night. Longer, untimed naps can also make you feel drowsier throughout the day. Although, there are some studies which show that people who are used to taking regular naps do not experience poor or disturbed sleep quality at night. So this just shows that if your body is used to the regulated rest during the day, then you won't be experiencing the ill effects of sleep deprivation at night. This theory boils down to the individual.

Keep a constant, fixed time.

It is very important to set a time frame for your rest and stick to it. Your inner circadian rhythm works on a set loop, working your body up at sunrise and winding down during sunset. Being consistent with your sleep and waking up schedule can help you improve your sleep pattern in the long run. If you have difficulties sleeping, you should try to adapt yourself to the natural daylight rhythm and shut off most light as the day progresses to night. It will take time for your body to adjust back to the natural circadian rhythm, but it is not impossible. Try getting into the habit of going to bed and waking up at the same time every day. After a couple of weeks, you will notice a stark difference in your sleep schedule, and you won't even need an alarm to wake you up.

These are some useful tips for if you are struggling to fall asleep or having trouble keeping a fixed time to get to bed.

VII
Effects of Positive Experiences on Stress Levels

Introduction

Positive affect defines an individual's inclination towards positive emotions and the way to interact with challenges in a positive way. On the contrary, the negative effect involves experiencing the world in a negative way, getting negative emotions, and more negativity in relationships and surroundings. Thus the two states can drastically affect the thinking capability of an individual. A person can be highly positive and highly negative at the same time. Therefore the amount of stress that a person takes depends upon the thinking pattern.

Relation between positive affect and stress

Positive affect can be directly linked to the characteristics of people who tend to be happier, optimistic, and successful. However, many people mistakenly consider the positive effect a by-product of happiness and a less stressful life. It is true that positive experiences can bring down stress levels in the human body. However, it isn't true that who has everything to be happy about is a positive thinking person and is less stressed.

A famous psychologist Barbara Fredrickson has deeply researched the effects of positive experiences on stress and has introduced a model about the impact of positive thinking on resilience. This model is known as the "Broaden and Build" theory of positive psychology.

The researcher has established that when we lift our mood, our perspective expands, and we are able to notice more possibilities in our lives. Thus positive thinking empowers us to utilize the following resources effectively.

Physical Resources

Suppose you are in a good mood. You will be in a better situation to tackle things in life and enhance your physical resources. The physical resources include energy, stamina, fitness, health, and wellness.

Psychological Resources

Suppose you are experiencing more positive effects. You might be less prone to entertain negative thoughts and start focusing on productive possibilities in life. The psychological resources include selecting optimistic ways, driving back yourself from deep thinking, and sustaining hectic schedules without experiencing a brain drain.

Social Resources

Social resources mean the human surrounding is supportive, from family to friends. These people will give you constructive suggestions when you tell them about your problem. Thus if you are in a negative mind-set condition, talking to these people will eventually help you in solving the issue you are facing.Positive affect can be a ladder for achieving the most difficult things in life.

On the contrary, if you are negative, it can also have a similar effect on your mind-set and directly affect your positive mood and pleasure in life. Thus the impact of positive experiences in life will develop a positive attitude and enhance your resilience towards stress.

Different Ways to increase positive experiences in your life.

The great thing about positive affect is that it can be created and further cultivated to gain motivation in life. The effectiveness of the positive effect is inborn, meaning people have a greater proclivity towards being in a good mood. For staying in a good mood, you can perform different things. Some of the things which can germinate a good mood in your brain are mentioned below.

Engaging yourself in Hobbies

As human beings, we all have certain hobbies. Your hobbies might differ from others, but you should still pursue them because pursuing what you like to do can help you cut off from all the stress in your life. Moreover, it will also help you in releasing toxicity from your body.

Do regular exercise

Like it or not, physical exercising every day can drastically reduce the stress levels in your body. When you perform the physical workout, the heart starts pumping more blood to your brain, the breathing changes as you take more oxygen into your system. Thus, the stress levels will be reduced. Moreover, it isn't necessary that for doing physical exercise you need a gym. You can perform a physical workout by getting involved in sports you like the most every day.

Get involved in life pleasures

Always focus on doing things you feel will give you pleasure in life. Generally, the majority of people like traveling and exploring new places. If you are in the same category, getting new joys in life will be easy. Our mind is dynamic and gets bored very quickly; thus, it is necessary that we keep it fresh by doing tasks that well like to do the most.

Practice Meditation

If you want to know the effects of meditation, listen to people who are sports personalities. Most of the players in sports face constant pressure and feel weighted the majority time of the year. Famous sports personalities have said that meditation has helped them extensively in stress management. Even the researchers say the same because your breathing style changes with meditation, and your focus increases.

Conclusion

In this article, we have thoroughly explained the effect of positive experiences on maintaining stress levels. While explaining the concept, we have explained the relation between positive thinking and stress. In addition, we have also described the different ways you can experience positive affect in life.

VIII

6 Best Nootropics supplements to boost brain power

Introduction

Nootropics, also known as smart drugs, can enhance brain performance. These drugs are also called cognition enhancers or memory-enhancing substances. When a doctor prescribes a person to consume nootropics medications that have stimulant effects. The patient can overcome medical conditions such as deficit hyperactivity disorder (ADHD), narcolepsy, or Alzheimer's.

Moreover, some non-prescribed substances are also considered for enhancing brain performance, such as caffeine and creatine. These substances don't treat diseases, but they might have some effects on thinking, memory, and other mental functions.

In this article, we will mention some nootropics supplements which are beneficial for brain function in healthy people. These nootropics will increase cognitive function, memory, motivation, alertness, and creativity. Some of the best nootropics supplements are:-

Fish oil

Fish oil is an excellent source of docosahexaenoic (DHA) and eicosapentaenoic acid (EPA), which are two types of omega-3 fatty acids. These fatty acids are linked to different health benefits, including brain health.

DHA plays a vital role in creating a balance between the structure and function of your brain. DHA contributes around 25 % of the total fat and approximately 90 % of the total omega-3 fat found in the brain cells. EPA, the other omega-3 fatty acid in fish oil, has anti-inflammatory effects that protect the brain from getting damaged and aging.

According to scientists, consuming DHA supplements directly affects thinking skills, memory, and reaction time in healthy people who have low DHA intakes. Moreover, it also assists people experiencing a decline in brain function.

Resveratrol

Resveratrol is a natural antioxidant found in fruits that are either purple or red in color, such as grapes, blueberries, raspberries. Astonishingly it is also found red wine and chocolates as well. According to research, it has been found that consuming resveratrol supplements can prevent the deterioration of the hippocampus, which is an essential part of the brain. Hippocampus is a part of the brain which affects human memory.

If the consumption of resveratrol is so beneficial, then it can reduce the declination speed of brain function with age. Moreover, animal studies have found out that resveratrol contributes to the betterment of memory and brain function. But, there are not enough human studies that show that resveratrol affects the thinking power of the human brain.

Creatine

Creatine is a significant contributor to the energy metabolism. The substance is found naturally in the human body, mainly in the muscles and even in smaller amounts in the brain. Creatine is a famous supplement, but you can get an ample amount of the substance from different animal products like meat, fish, and eggs. Creatine can increase the thinking capability of the people who don't meat.

Caffeine

Caffeine is a stimulant which is found in tea and coffee. When a person consumes caffeine, it stimulates the brain and central nervous system, which makes the person feel less tired and more alert. Moreover, studies have concluded that caffeine can make you feel more energized and improve your memory, reaction time, and general brain functions.

The amount of caffeine present in one cup of coffee varies, but generally, it is 50-400mg. For the majority of people, the safe consumption of caffeine is around 200-400mg per day, and this quantity is enough for them to maintain good health. A person consuming caffeine should avoid its overdosage because consuming more caffeine can cause anxiety, nausea in trouble sleeping.

Phosphatidylserine

Phosphatidylserine is a kind of fat compound known as a phospholipid found in the brain. Expert nutritionists say that consuming phosphatidylserine cab be highly fruitful in maintaining brain health. Moreover, studies have shown that consuming 100 mg of phosphatidylserine three times a day can help a person in countering the age-related decline in brain function.

Moreover, in people who consume 400 mg of phosphatidylserine supplements, their thinking skills and memory have improved. However, more research still needs to be conducted in this domain for recognizing the effects of phosphatidylserine.

Acetyl-L-Carnitine

Acetyl-L-Carnitine is a type of amino acid that is produced naturally in the human body. This supplement plays an essential role in enhancing metabolism, especially energy production. According to researchers, consuming acetyl-L-carnitine supplements can help you in feeling more alert, improving memory and memory loss which is linked to aging.

The effect of acetyl-L-carnitine supplements has been observed in animals. In animals, it has been shown that the substance reduces the decline in brain function and increases learning capacity. Moreover, in humans, the studies have found that the compound is a valuable supplement for slowing the decline in brain function due to aging. Furthermore, the consumption of acetyl-L-carnitine can also help you in improving people against mild dementia and Alzheimer's.

IX
5 Ways to Refresh and Rest Your Mind

Introduction

Human life today has become hectic when compared to the early 90s. Thus, when you have hustled all day long or a week, refreshing your brain with the help of gadgets seems highly likely. However, this is not the right approach for keeping your mind fresh. To keep your mind fresh, you need to release all the stress and pressure present in your brain. Because staying under pressure for a longer duration of time drains your cognitive ability and brain activity. Thus staying under constant pressure directly affects your personal lives, relationship, and career.

If anyone reading this article is in the same boat and is looking out for ways to energize your mind and refresh your brain, then in this article, we will be mentioning a few ways which can help you build a healthy mind for a long duration of time.

Focus on taking deep breaths

It is scientifically proven that a person who practices deep breathing notices a significant reduction in stress levels. According to scientists, practicing deep breathing animates the wandering nerve in the body. At this point, the nerve develops an anti-stress synthetic called acetylcholine. The compound is the primary synapse of our parasympathetic framework that develops calmness in our body and relaxes our mind.

For beginning deep breathing, you can start in the following way.

Rest or plunk down, keep the back straight and keep your hands on the stomach.

After getting into the initial position, draw full breath with the aim that your belly pushes out.

Once you have taken a deep breath, hold the breath for 5 seconds and then slowly exhale.

For observing positive effects, practice deep breathing a few times a day.

Go for a short walk down the street

.

When you are sitting idle, the body is at rest. Hence, the system feels low, and thus the brain activity decreases. However, when you move your body, the mitochondria create energy which the body requires. Therefore you feel more energetic.

Scientists say that with regular physical activity, the number of mitochondria in the body increases by two folds. Hence, more energy is produced by the body. Moreover, the flow of fresh air transforms the blood flow. It refreshes the human mind, which ultimately lowers stress levels. One of the good ways to keep your mind fresh is by taking a walk for a couple of days in the entire week.

Therefore, if you feel stressed, taking a walk down the street can help you refresh your mind and soul.

Drinking ample amount of water

Drinking an equal quantity of water throughout the day can help you rejuvenate the mind. Especially one glass of water just after waking up helps drastically. Below when you sleep, the fluid intake of the body is zero. Therefore, if you drink water just after getting up from the bed, it helps in the proper functioning of the brain cells.

75 % of the brain is the result of water. Thus, if we aren't hydrated in the right way, our cerebrum works sluggishly due to the lack of the driving force. Hence in such situations, we feel stressed and experience weakness. Thus, to refresh your mind and stimulate your brain cells, it is essential to drink ample water.

Use Heating Pads

Heating pads can be an excellent way to reduce the stress levels in our bodies. When you place the heating pad on a specific part of your body, the blood flow increases in the area because of an increase in temperature. Thus exposing the stressed area to heat increases the blood flow; therefore, the stress levels decrease, and we feel calmed down. Moreover, providing heat to a particular part increases muscle adaptability.

Eat Nutritious food

"You are what you eat" it's an extremely well-said quote. If you eat junk, you will always feel lethargic and radiate negative energy. However, if you eat healthily, your brain will function well, and you will feel energetic all day long because eating nutritious food will fulfill your need for glucose which is the primary source of energy in the body.

You should have a diet in which you eat an ample amount of nuts, seeds, and dried organic products, which are recommended in your area. Moreover, you can keep a box of nuts next to you while working and munch them when you feel hungry. Moreover, while eating proper meals, you should focus on eating green vegetables, fruits, etc.

Avoid eating food that contain high sugar because eating sugary food will drastically increase the glucose level in the body, which will make you initially feel energetic but afterward, you will feel drained. Hence while eating meals, make sure that you focus on eating healthy food. Make a comprehensive diet plan containing proteins and sugar in equal proportion according to your preferences and focus on taking small portions of meals.

"Do not wait to strike till the iron is hot; but make it hot by striking." - William Butler Yeats

X

6 Ways to Relax More Effectively

"This world is too short to enjoy", said some unknown genius. But is it really so? Even though actions speak louder than words and even though we strive everyday to try to achieve our goals, I don't agree with the unknown genius completely, because every once in a while, it is always good to stop, relax, enjoy the scenery around you, and then continue. Don't you think that working anytime and every time is not just unhealthy but also counter-productive as studies have shown?

There are lots of different and unique ways to relax effectively and recharge your tirelessly working mind and body. Ranging from your family doctor to the opinions of different people on the internet, there are various ways to relax effectively both your biceps and cerebrum.

Food: One of the best methods and one of the popular methods of relaxation. That's because when we eat, our brain secretes endorphins which are responsible for reducing the feeling of pain. Endorphins are also the hormones which make you feel better. Therefore, whenever you are feeling tired or low, go eat that delicious chocolate bar, or go dig into that pizza. Eating crunchy food is also preferred although you can even eat mangoes or drink honey, basically anything that's a little sweet. Although potato chips are quite a favorite too. Right after you've eaten your favorite delicacy, trust me, you'll feel more refreshed and relaxed and hence, ready to go on.

Inner peace: Another very important factor that plays an important role in deciding how tired or relaxed you feel at any given time is your inner peace. There are quite a few methods to achieve that 'monk-like' peace.

Meditation: Just close your eyes, sit in a comfortable posture and just breath while concentrating on a particular thing.

Just letting your head rest on the pillow also plays wonders.

Breathe: This might seem too simple, but trust me, just taking a long breath can help release all that burden you've been feeling all this while.

Creative visualization: We all day-dream. And that's another very good way to release stress and relax. Just imagining yourself in a happy situation actually helps you relax better.

Nap: Although not much appreciated by the lecturers and bosses, a quick nap can play wonders as a relaxation technique and would help your mind to feel refreshed.

Just keeping your eyes closed without actually sleeping is also another option.

Massage: Gently massaging your arms or having a full body massage is a good recovery technique to relax the muscles of the body.

Some techniques like 'acupressure' and 'acupuncture'.

Squeezing that smiley faced yellow ball also relaxes your brain indefinitely.

Just dripping cold water on your wrists or behind the earlobes also keeps the brain from tensing a lot and hence relax it.

Repetitive actions like brushing your hair or knitting also help.

Environment: This is as important as one's inner peace. Naturally, 'what surrounds one, affects one'. Therefore,

Take time to be alone. Being in your own company is one of the best relaxation techniques.

Maintain a 'Zen-zone', a place where you would go, to feel better, or to better your mood.

Sunlight: There's no better feeling than waking up to a sunny morning. Bright light stimulates hormones which make us joyful and happy. Sunbathing will definitely help you feel better and immensely relaxed.

Gazing out the window: Simple task such as these reap amazing results. Looking out of the window and watching the lush green of grass or watching birds fly are some tasks to relax the brain and help one feel a lot better

Organizing: Keeping those pens in the pen stand and arranging your books or pile of papers neatly can have quite drastic effects on feeling good. That is why it is a good and even an encouraged practice to make one's bed after getting up.

Exercise: A healthy and relaxed mind is often found in a healthy body. Taking time to exercise is quite an important practice and should be inculcated in one's daily lifestyle. The different forms of exercises which help in relaxation are:

Yoga: a powerful tool to keep one's mind and body healthy.

Stretching one's body.

Going for a walk in the morning or during the evening.

A good jog early in the morning is the way to set one's day.

Entertainment and Creativity:

Netflix and chill: There's no better feeling than sitting in bed munching nachos while watching your favorite TV show. This right here is what relaxation is; chilling that's what it is.

Memes: These are an integral part of our lives and as such the only reason majority of people use Social networking apps.

Watching comedies: Laughing keeps us hale and hearty.

Hobbies: Doing what you like will make you feel quite happy. Be it singing or dancing or playing a guitar, do what most excites you and you will definitely relax.

Solve a puzzle: Putting your brain to work in such a way would help your case. So, try solving that crossword puzzle in today's paper and some problems on integral calculus while you're at it. Just kidding.

Jot down all that happened during the day in your journal or diary.

Read some good novel and disappear into the fabulous fictional world offered by the writers and taste bliss.

Socializing: Human being has been and will continue to be a social animal. It is only natural when a person feels comfortable and relaxed in the company of his/her friends.

Talk to a friend: call him/her up, talk for hours together, discuss your problems and talk about the Manchester derby. Anything that will make you feel better. Also, not just your friends, call mom and dad, tell them how's everything; and trust me you'll never feel better than that.

Laugh: Crack jokes, laugh at other's jokes; be happy, keep others happy.

Plan that long-awaited vacation to Goa or Ladakh or even Winterfell, basically wherever you want to go.

"Growth begins when we start to accept our own weaknesses." - Jean Vanier

XI
7 Ways to Avoid Overthinking

Introduction

Overthinking is a common problem which is faced by people these days. However, before countering the problem, we first need to understand what overthinking is. Because once you know about overthinking, you will be in a better place for countering it. Thus, you will know the pattern and eventually help yourself improve your mental health.

Overthinking is often defined as a human reaction to abide by something excessively. When a person overthinks about a particular thing, the mind is stuck in a never-ending loop that generates thoughts about a problem that doesn't even exist.

Thinking about dilemmas, problems, and decisions when you are awake is the reaction of a normal person. But thinking about your problems outside the working hours can create various symptoms such as anxiety and depression. In this article, we will explain 7 ways a person can avoid overthinking.

Focus on learning mindfulness skills

A person who is a master of mindfulness meditation can control stress, enhance optimism, feel relaxed, counter anxiety issues, and much more. Moreover, suppose a person is capable of staying in the present. In that case, the skill can massively assist him in detecting ruminations and worrying thoughts without judgment. Moreover, if a person stays in the present, controlling negative thoughts and getting rid of the negative thoughts also becomes easy.

Expel Perfectionism

Having goals and aspirations in life is completely fine. But there is a thin line between healthy striving and perfectionism. A person who excessively focuses on becoming perfect is highly vulnerable to developing insecurity and fear. Because perfectionism doesn't lead a person towards problem-solving and bigger achievements. A perfectionist doesn't have realistic goals and often works upon unworkable ambitions.

Perfectionist is harsh on themselves if they make a mistake and are extremely critical about everything. Moreover, chasing perfectionism can lead you to anxiety, depression, and addiction. A common trait observed in perfectionists is their high focus on mistakes and not on accomplishments. Thus, instead of chasing perfectionism, a person should focus on distinguishing between realistic and unrealistic goals, which will eventually help him achieve productive things in life.

Examine the realistic scope of the situation

A person going through overthinking will do excessive rumination and get insecure by the results, which doesn't even exist. If a person gets involved in extreme rumination, they suffer from mood, health, and relationship problems. A person should smartly identify the rumination and find what triggered it to avoid extreme rumination. Also, a person who is constantly overthinking should stop and think about the evidence, which creates a negative mindset.

Thus a person who chooses to solve a problem instead of abiding by the challenges can easily overcome overthinking.

Have faith in your intuition

Before taking the final step in a crucial decision, many famous and renowned people don't think about it deeply. Instead, they trust their knowledge and follow their gut feeling. Following gut feeling can provide you with creative solutions and allow you to see things from different perspectives.

However, most of us ignore the intuition we receive while facing a problem. Suppose a person follows his intuition, then it can better understand themselves, enhance their optimism, and reduce stress and anxiety levels caused due to overthinking.

Designate time for self-reflection every day

Getting lost in your negative thoughts is very easy. Thus to avoid such a situation, a person should try practicing mindfulness. Moreover, a person should also learn to acknowledge their thoughts when they become pessimistic. Furthermore, they should also focus on the emotions that developed such thoughts in their brain.

To know all the details concerned with a negative thought, a person needs to designate a particular time of the day in their routine for self-reflection.

Focus on moving forward

Many people have the habit of constantly thinking about the past and figuring out if they could have taken a particular step, the result would've been different. However, thinking about the past is not going to change it.

Constantly thinking about the possibilities of the past can only make a person anxious, depressed, and face other mental issues.

Thus, every time you start to think about the possibilities in the past, consider them as non-productive. Rather focus on practicing self-compassion and making peace with the mistakes of the past. Because when you make peace with the mistakes of the past, you become mentally stronger.

Focus on noticing when you overthink

Whenever you start to overthink, keeping track of the ruminations and the triggering element can prove to be extremely productive. Mindfulness can enhance the awareness of an unproductive path of thinking. Thus mindfulness actually helps you switch your mindset and pause overthinking. Moreover, once you know what triggers overthinking, your mind will help you in finding ways to tackle it. Hence, you might eventually get a solution for overthinking.

"Your life does not get better by chance, it gets better by change." - Jim Rohn

XII

Meditation

Wondering why people focus on meditation so much? Want to know the benefits of meditation and how long do you need to meditate regularly? We have got answers to all your questions.

Meditation not only wipes stress but also brings inner peace. Lately, if you have been anxious, worried, and tense then you should give meditation a try. Spending some time in the quiet meditating can not only restore your inner calm but also your peace and help you settle within. The impressive factor about meditation is it doesn't cost you and it is very accessible, i.e. anybody can sit for meditation to relax and calm their body and mind. In addition to that, anyone can practice meditation anywhere. You can find your inner calm and peace regardless of the place you are in neither does it require any additional requirement.

What is meditation?

Meditation has been practiced by people for centuries. It has been originally developed and practiced to help people understand the mystical forces and sacred meaning of life. Currently, meditation has been the most popular means to achieve relaxation and de-stress people off their worry, tension and anxiety. This mind-body complementary medicine is known to provide a tranquil mind and deep relaxation after the activity has been performed successfully.

The procedure of meditation allows you to eliminate jumbled and haphazard thoughts which are believed to be crowding your mind and taking up all the space inside. The same jumbled thoughts if stay in your mind for long, will cause you stress which could have an impact on your body as well.

Benefits of meditation

By performing meditation you are not only achieving mental peace and inner calm but also focusing on achieving overall physical well-being. Now, here's the fun fact, even though you have performed meditation these benefits will remain with you and help you engage better throughout the day even after you have ended your session. By meditation for some time every morning, you can achieve a calmer and more peaceful day with your mind remaining relaxed and your body running energetically the entire day.

The relationship of Meditation and emotional well-being

Every time you decide to sit to meditate for a couple of minutes, you are ensuring that all your thoughts are steering clear and become organized in your mind. Throughout the process, you calm yourself down by throwing away the extra information which is creating a burden on your mind. Every day due to an overload of emotion and information, your mind and body generate stress which by the end of the week could be overwhelming and reach the saturation level.

There are several emotional benefits of performing meditation regularly for a couple of minutes including gaining better and new perspectives on how to tackle stressful events and situations. In addition to that, you also develop skills that will prepare you to better react to stress healthily. You also increase your self-awareness and start to remain attentive and focused on the present rather than dwelling about the past or worrying about the future.

Meditating regularly also keeps your negative emotions and energy in check while enhancing and increasing the creativity and imagination of your mind. Last but not the least, it helps you to increase your tolerance level and patience which are quite important in today's fast leading lives.

Meditation and its effect on different illnesses

If you have a stress-induced medical condition, then you should consider meditating regularly even more. There are several studies and pieces of research done around meditation that suggest that it supports the health benefits. But on the other hand, there is still some confusion as to whether meditation has any medical benefits or not. While having that in mind, here are some illnesses which is known to be cured or manageable if patients perform meditation regularly.

Several illnesses including anxiety, asthma, chronic pain, depression, high blood pressure, heart diseases, and even sleep and headache issues are believed to be made manageable through regular meditation sessions. Although it is advised to consult your doctor before you start meditating to receive educated advice.

Different types of meditation to choose from

There are different kinds of meditation to choose from including guided meditation, mindfulness meditation, mantra meditation, tai chi, and Qi gong. The differences lie in visualization, repetition of calming words, physical movement while relaxing, and even being present while performing meditation. Even yoga is considered a type of meditation that involves several different postures and breathing exercises that calm your mind and body.

The main elements of meditation are attention, relaxation, breathing, and a quiet and peaceful setting. The elements vary in severity depending on the kind of meditation you are performing. Meditation is very efficient, essential and beneficial for people who lead a high-performing and busy lifestyle daily.

XIII

10 Most Powerful Meditation Techniques to Gain Mental Strength Fast

Back a decade ago if one would have said this as a statement with answers, then all people would have considered the individual as a retarded who needs special attention. But now this statement has taken up a form of a question that everyone is seeking answers for because there is so much on the other side if mental strength isn't good enough. These days' people are taking up medications and other types of help so that they can have good mental strength and this is not a lie; it's the truth. In this fast-paced world, everyone is working so much hard so that they can secure their future up to point where they just stop doing everything sit back & relax, but they don't find that point they just keep doing work & staking up money in the accounts for a time which will never come if they keep on going like this.

Why does the mental strength matters so much- Below are the few points which will shed some light that why is mental strength so important-

• Productivity & efficiency gets affected due to weak mental strength

• One might win in the current scenario, but they are losing in the long run

• It also welcomes diseases which one can't spot coming & after some time they become incurable.

• One might do best on this day but the day after tomorrow will be worst & then followed by a series of unfortunate & incurable events.

• The mental ability also causes Glucose Metabolism, Heart conditions & type 2 Diabetes risk

• Depression & mental disorder.

What should be done to get a good mental strength- Below are some of the proven meditation techniques which will help in building a good mental strength-

• Get rid of the negative thoughts- One should be optimistic in every situation possible doesn't matter the type of situation. Being always negative isn't making things to turn out good, in fact, it is worsening it up.

• Find a way- There is always a way out and if necessary one should take it. Controlling the uncontrollable is just pushing one down. So don't try to control things which are way out of reach.

• Start with a bang but don't end it with a fuss- One should always start the day by doing the stuff they like it doesn't matter if it's out of place. It can be drinking coffee, running, exercising, etc.

• Adopt new habits- either its cleaning the room, gardening, swimming because these things don't require one to sit & think instead one has to put the effort in all these. It will take time because the brain isn't ready for this but make it ready to be well prepared.

• Don't let one failure affect the routine- If one has skipped some daily routine that doesn't mean that all day time table is unbalanced, it's all in mind. So be well prepared for everything if one activity is skipped or missed doesn't matter so balance the time adjust the body according to it.

• One should do what they love not what they are told- Everyone is different nobody is the same, so why do what others are doing. One should make their own routine instead of doing the same universal routine.

• Just start with a simple meditation- Meditation is an art not some crash course so take it as an art, practice it. Start with time-bound meditation and then let go of the time just be in the mood.

• Find love in everything- Don't force anything just find something in it will let one stick around it. Like if one is skipping sleep just because they want to do meditation, it wouldn't work. So don't see a task see it as an opportunity.

• Quantity and quality of eating matters -If one has carved for junk food & sugary products then they have to take some serious decisions like replace all that with fresh substitutes & change the time of taking meals because the impact of meditation also depends on the type of food.

• Monitor the work- Keeping track of the progress will surely help one to feel happy and that's the primary goal of meditation. As depending on the progress, one should also increase the time of meditation.

XIV
10 Myths Of Self Hypnosis

Hypnosis is something that has gained a lot of popularity in the recent years, it is mainly because of its portrayal in many movies and TV shows. Hypnosis has been used for generations as a therapeutic medicine. It has been used by yogis, and other monks to help others and help themselves. Today, we will discuss some of the top 10 myths that are floating around about self hypnosis.

I will lose my mind if I try self hypnosis.

Well, the first one is one of the most important ones that have to be talked about. It is not like how it is described in movies and TV shows, when you are hypnotized, you will not be losing your mind. In fact, you will be fully aware of everything that is happening around you. You can always come out of the trance state as long as you have control of whatever is happening to you.

I will be stuck in a trance state forever.

This is again another myth. Hypnosis is a state that is naturally occurring, meaning that you can never get stuck in a trance state for ever. You can always come out of the trance state that you have been put in or that you have put yourself in by opening your eyes.

I will have no idea about what is going on around me when I am self hypnotized.

Again, this is a popular but completely untrue myth. Many scientific studies have shown that people are actually in a more alert state when they are under hypnosis, meaning that their senses are heightened and they can definitely, and in fact sense the things around them even better.

Self Hypnosis is not meant for all people.

Actually, speaking self hypnosis is best suited for the people who are sound psychologically and who are not actively suffering from any kind of mental diseases or disorders. This is essentially a process where you are going to reassure yourself that everything will be fine. This actually increases the efficiency and the productivity as well as the confidence of the person.

Self hypnosis is meant only for the people who have weak minds.

Self hypnosis is meant for people who are actually above than the rest of the people when it comes to intelligence as well as creativity. It is shown that people who have better focus and concentration are very good subjects when they are hypnotized.

Self Hypnosis is a complicated procedure.

Self hypnosis may seem like a complicated thing for people who are trying it for the first time. But in reality, there is nothing very complex about the whole procedure. Unlike other treatments that are there, you do not need to visit a hospital or take any pills so it is much simple and much safer as well. All you need is someone you trust or if you are going to self hypnotize, you do not need anyone else to look after you.

Self hypnotism is contrary to many religious beliefs.

Self hypnosis is not related to any region that is present anywhere in the world. Many religions like Buddhism, Christianity, Hinduism or even Judaism allow its followers to use or get hypnosis treatments done. No professional hypnotist will ever try to change or question your religious beliefs even if you are in a trance state, because it is not ethical nor is it professional behavior.

Self hypnosis is expensive to learn and perform.

There are ways that you can learn to self hypnotize yourself if you do not want to see a psychiatrist or a hypnosis specialist for whatever the reason. Besides, hypnosis can be a better way to calm down your mood than many of the dangerous and expensive pills that are available in the market. When you consider all the side effects of the pills that you could consume instead of self hypnotising, you will be better off with self hypnotising. Besides, self hypnotising is a one time investment and will serve you for the rest of your life.

I will be vulnerable when I am under self hypnosis.

When hypnosis is conducted in a safe environment there is absolutely nothing for you to worry about. Besides when you are self hypnotising yourself there is no one else that is involved in the process for you to even feel vulnerable. You are in complete control of what you do or what you say when you are in a trance state.

Self hypnosis is just sleep.

Well, though many people feel tried after hypnosis, they are alert when they are under hypnosis. This effectively means that there is no one to restrict you or disturb you in your healing process. People may fall asleep after they are done with their hypnosis, which is quite common especially with new people who are trying it out.

XV

12 High Energy Foods to Increase Your Mental Health.

Food is something that most of us enjoy, not only does it provide the nourishment that we require on a daily basis, it is also responsible for keeping us healthy and fit. Our mind is our greatest resource. If we are to take care of our body, we must also take care of our mind. And that is why mental health foods are important. This article focuses on 12 high energy foods that will do wonders for your mental health. So, keep reading to know how to have a stronger and better mental health.

Walnuts

Well, nuts are a favorite snack for many people. Walnuts are one of the best snacks that can help you keep your mind fit. Walnuts are shaped like the brain. So, it will always be easy for you to remember why they are special. Walnuts are a superfood that contains a very high amount of Omega 3 fatty acid. These are the things that help you keep your mind fit by helping your mind remember things in a better way. Walnuts are very important, especially if you are a student. So, munch down on a few when you are studying.

Fish (Fatty)

Fish is considered brain food. Fish has a very high content of something that scientists call DHA which is again a type of Omega 3 fatty acid. This acid has been proven to help mental health by reducing the levels of anxiety in the human brain. A less stressed mind is a better mind and fish helps to achieve this. Salmon, prawns, or pretty much most seafood have good amounts of DHA. So, don't be shy to take some servings of fish on a regular basis.

Green Leafy vegetables.

Everyone must have seen the TV show Popeye, where he eats tons of spinach to get stronger. The catch is that leafy green vegetables like spinach not only do wonders for your physical health, they also help a lot in keep your mind at ease. They have high levels of vitamin B as well as folic acid. These are known to help people cope up with depression, insomnia and also the fatigue of daily life.

Yogurt.

Granted yogurt is a yummy dessert that most people cannot get enough of. There is another reason for all of you who are like this. Fermented food like yogurt has been shown to reduce stress hormones as well as anxiety in human beings. So, not only are your taste buds happy, but your brain is also happy and healthy because of consuming yogurt. The main source of this goodness is because of something that we call probiotics, that active cultured yogurt has a lot of.

Protein (Lean).

Proteins, especially thin ones are very helpful in helping curb depression. This is also emphasized by the fact that lean proteins are often called the Prozac that is natural. Lean meats like chicken, beans, turkey, and eggs have a lot of good effects on your body and help you improve your mental health.

Almonds.

Everyone loves almonds; they can be had salted, unsalted, mixed with other nuts and so on. It is a known fact that almonds are helpful in making people remember things better. That is probably one of the reasons why you can see students snacking on a bag of almonds while studying.

Coffee.

Do not be surprised when you find coffee on the list. Caffeine is the main ingredient in coffee, that is what keeps you awake in the morning, and that is what helps you to feel lesser stress.

Blueberries.

Blueberries have the ability to give a compound called anthocyanins to your brain. These are compounds which have anti-inflammatory as well as antioxidant effects — these actions against the stress as well as inflammation in the body and the mind.

Turmeric.

Turmeric contains an active ingredient that is called 'curcumin.' This has been shown to be able to cross the blood-brain barrier. In effect, this means that turmeric can go directly to the brain and help heal the cells directly.

Pumpkin seeds.

Pumpkin seeds have been shown to keep the brain free from the things that can cause radical brain damage. They contain very powerful anti-oxidants that can do this job for you.

Dark Chocolate.

Cocoa powder, as well as dark chocolate, are full of some boosting compounds for your brain. These include caffeine, anti-oxidants as well as flavonoids. These flavonoids are from a group of plant compounds that are anti-oxidant.

Oranges.

Oranges mainly have Vitamin C. now; Vitamin C helps keep the brain healthy because it is an important factor in keeping mental decline in check, especially in older people. It has been shown that eating enough oranges can protect the person from Alzheimer's disease.

"The road to success is always under construction." - Lily Tomlin

XVI

Best Music and Tones for your Brain

Introduction

The best music and tines for your brain are the isochronic tones. The isochronic tones are used in the process of brain wave entertainment. Brain wave entertainment refers to getting brain waves to sync with a specific stimulus. The stimulus is generally audio or visual.

Brain wave entertainment techniques, for instance, the isochronic tones, are being studied extensively to cure several mental diseases such as pain, a deficit of hyperactivity disorder, and anxiety.

Description about Isochronic tones

Isochronic tones are the tones that are generated regularly in evenly spaced intervals. The interval is typically very brief, which creates a rhythmic pulse. The isochronic tones are generally present in music and natural sounds.

Isochronic tones help in brain wave entertainment. In brain wave entertainment, your brain waves sync with the frequency you are listening to. According to studies, it is believed that the syncing of brain waves to a certain frequency might help you in inducing different mental states. The brain waves are produced by electrical activity in the brain, and they can be easily measured with the help of EEG.

There are different types of brain waves. Each type of brain wave is associated with a frequency range and a mental state. The brain waves are mentioned below

Gamma

Beta

Alpha

Theta

Delta

Comparison between Isochronic, binaural and monaural waves

There might be a scenario where you might have heard about the other different waves, such as binaural and monaural beats. Compared to isochronic tones, the binaural and monaural beats are continuous. Meaning the tones don't turn on or off, as with isochronic tones. Moreover, the waves are also generated differently.

Binaural Beats

Binaural waves are produced when two waves of different frequencies are presented to each ear. The difference between the frequencies is processed inside our brain. For instance, a 330Hz beat is supplied to your left ear while a 300Hz beat is supplied to the right ear. Then the 30Hz difference is processed by the brain. Thus a Binaural beat will be best experienced with the help of headphones.

Monaural Beats

Monaural beats are generated when two similar beats are combined and then presented to either one of the ears. Like binaural tones, you can easily perceive the difference between the two frequencies as a beat. Since the two frequencies are combined before listening, you can listen to these tones on speakers and don't necessarily need headphones.

Benefits of listening to Waves

According to studies, it is concluded that the isochronic tones and other forms of brain wave entertainment can stimulate certain mental states. Thus listening to such waves can be beneficial for several purposes, such as

Enhancement in attention

Improvement in sleep

Releasing the stress and anxiety levels.

Handling pain

Improving memory

Meditation

Mood enhancement

According to different researches, it has been concluded that lower frequency brain waves such as theta and delta waves are linked to the sleep state. Thus, hearing a low-frequency isochronic wave can help you promote better sleep.

The higher frequency waves, such as the gamma and the beta waves, are linked to the active and engaged mind. Therefore listening to these high-frequency isochronic tones can possibly help inattentiveness and concentration.

The other wave, the alpha wave, is an intermediate brain wave that can help you in a relaxed state. Therefore listening to isochronic tones with the alpha wave frequency can help you relax and aid meditation.

Research on Binaural waves

The research was conducted in the year 2019. The research was focused on finding the effects of binaural beats in 32 participants. The participants were made to listen to binaural beta or theta waves, which are generally associated with the active mind, sleep or tiredness.

Once the participants had heard the waves, they were asked to recall the tasks. From the experiment, it was observed that the people who listened to binaural waves in the beta range were able to recall more words correctly than those who were exposed to binaural waves in the theta range.

Moreover, in 2018 a study of how low-frequency binaural beats affected the sleep of 24 participants was conducted. The binaural beats were used in the delta range, linked to deep sleep.

The result of the study showed that the duration of deep sleep was more in the participants who listened to the binaural beats compared to those who didn't. Moreover, these participants spent less time in light sleep.

Research on Monaural beats

The research was conducted in the year 2017. The research examined the effect of monaural beats on anxiety and cognition in 25 participants. The beats were introduced in theta, alpha and gamma ranges.

Researchers found that the monaural beats didn't have a considerable effect on the memory of the participants. However, a considerable amount of effect was observed on the anxiety levels of the individuals.

XVII

How Fear Affects the Growth of Your Personality

Fear has a lot of effects on our personality. Fear also makes us do many things that we don't want to do and stop us doing things that we really want to do. Everyone comes across the emotion of fear very often. Some people have the fear of the dark, some fear heights, flying and what not. But in a way, fear is necessary as it plays a very important role in it helps with career problem and relationship problems in people's lives. There are many unconscious fears as well which affects the decision-making process as it makes you incline towards the opposite side of the fear unconsciously and they also cause many emotional conflicts.

According to studies, some people have a greater tendency towards fear. They experience dear at a lower extent than others, it's just the way they are born. Overcoming fear is one of the greatest achievement you can get as it is not very easy. But in the process of overcoming fear, your personality will undergo many positive changes because you are fighting against an emotion which stops you from doing the thing that you really want to do. Which will lead to a more open-minded and strong personality because the one who can overcome his fears are capable of doing anything in the world because the main problem exists inside your head, ones you are got past that everything else is much simpler than you think.

Fear of Public Speaking

Some fears are unconscious which are conditioned because of family pressure and society's norms but there are developed fears as well. The fear that you developed from your childhood due to some incident also affects our personality. There are some fears that are just there like the fear of speaking in public which makes us do fewer things in public because of the fear in mind that 'what other people will think of me'. This is one of the most common fears in humans. It happens to everyone and it happens a lot. For example, when you are learning in a class filled with about 50 students and you had a doubt in some topic that is been taught in the class then the most obvious thing is to ask the teacher about that doubt. But the thoughts like what will others think of me, what if this is a stupid question and I am the only one who doesn't understand such a dumb thing? These thoughts are again the fear of 'what others will think of me'. This fear just puts you backward and affect your personality in a negative way because it just doesn't let you do things you want. Let's consider a person who doesn't have such a fear, he will ask that particular doubt in the class which will help him a lot in learning that faster and not only him it will also help other students who have this fear of not asking. If we look at some fears objectively they are just stupid. Like the one discussed above, why do you care what anyone else thinks about you, you are never gonna meet them and they can't affect your life in any way.

One of the most negative effects of fear on our personality is that it inhibits emotional growth and hence slowing down the process of maturing. It also causes stress, self-pity, unhappiness, unsatisfied and many other negative feelings.

Fear makes us feel Isolated

Fear also make you feel socially isolated. You might think why I am different than other and regardless of knowing that you are different, you are not trying to change because of your fear which again as discussed above, the fear inhibits your emotional growth. This also affects your relationship with your friends and family and results in depression and reclusiveness.

Embarrassment due to fear

Fear of something also causes embarrassment like what will you say when your friend asked why haven't you tried to ride a motorcycle or been on a plane. Telling them your fear will be too embarrassing for you. Fear of things like heights and dogs or motorcycles is really hard to manage because it comes with the underlying emotion of humiliation. And this embarrassment only promotes fear which affects your personality in a negative way.

Losing control of yourself

The out of control feeling is also associated with fear and it's one of the worst things. Whatever you try and do against your fear but you always seem to lose your control when encountering it. In a way, fear is driving you.

Helplessness due to fear

Some fears affect many aspects of your life like your career and personal life. You seem to feel helplessness. You want to make it all go away but it just doesn't.

It makes you a dull person and causes you to think the same for other aspects of life which results in conflicts in those aspects as well.

Fear of failure

The fear of failure, one more common fear among humans. There is a high chance that you have been a part of it too. This fear stops us from doing so many amazing things in life. What if I try to do this and I fail? my whole life can go in vain. This fear also lets us analyze our situation and can be helpful for us. It helps us see the future possibilities and help in decision making. This fear being helpful can also affect you in negative ways if it is employed too much. If you always think about failure, then you can't take one step forward because who knows what might kill you if you take a step ahead.

Everyone has some kind of fear wired inside them. But the one who overcomes their fear will become successful. Overcoming fear doesn't mean to completely vanish the fear from your system, it means that you should take advantages of your fear. Some people have suffered chronic fearful experiences due to which it's really hard on them to cope up with their fear but with proper treatment, it is possible to overcome that fear.

Live your life according to you, don't let your fear drive your life.

XVIII

How Prayer Affect your Well-Being and Success

Introduction

During difficult times, many people prefer to say prayers. Prayers have tremendous power when it comes to giving strength in difficult times. A person who speaks prayer doesn't feel lonely in a difficult time. The person seeks help from a higher power and finds the benefits of spirituality. Prayer not only provides you support during difficult times, but it also helps you get strong emotional health.

How do prayers affect the physical health of a person? Emotional health is an aspect that is highly affected when a person is suffering through a hard phase in life. In this article, we will address how prayers and spirituality protect emotional health.

Effect of prayers and spirituality on emotional and mental health

A person faces several challenges while studying the impact of prayer. These are the words of a renowned psychology professor from the University of Connecticut in Storrs. People who pray on a regular basis are active with the faith communities. Moreover, the people these people will also be able to make decisions that are healthy and towards the greater good.

There are several ways in which a regular spiritual practice might improve and protect emotional health.

Spiritual health offers provide a sense of purpose. Because spirituality helps you connect with greater power or truth, which provides you with a purpose or meaning beyond everyday activities.

Spirituality also provides social support to a person. According to a study, people with strong religious and spiritual lives maintained richer social connections. If you are spiritual, there are high chances that you meet people with a similar mindset.

People need a high spirit to tackle the situation during tough times, and spirituality provides that. During tough times you must have observed that spiritual people sing and chants mantras. The main idea behind the singing and chanting of mantras is to improve a person's emotional health. These mantras are filled with positive energy. When a person starts chanting it from their mouth, it directly sends a positive signal to the brain.

In difficult situations, spirituality or religion can provide a framework to deal with unexpected and adverse events. This is scientifically proven as well. It is seen that the people who regularly go to church have been observed with lesser symptoms of depression when dealing with a difficult situation such as the death of a loved one.

According to Park, "if you have faith, rely on it" and "if you don't, you can cultivate it." Some of the best ways to develop faith are by interacting with nature practicing yoga, or meditation. To generate faith, you can go to venues that provide you a sense of connection, unity and a feeling of peace.

The Health Benefits of prayer is real.

Many researchers have conducted real-time activities to determine the positive effects of spirituality on health. Some of the tests which are conducted are mentioned below.

Research conducted in 2015 on Health Psychology on 191 people with congestive health failure for five years found that out of the 191, the individuals who adopted a healthy lifestyle and spiritual peace were significantly more inclined to live a longer and healthier life in comparison to their peers.

Another research was conducted, and it mainly focused on major depressive disorder or chronic medical illness. According to the result published by this research, a person who showed religiosity, which contains regular religious experiences, was more optimistic than their peers.

A person who is fell into doing wrong deeds such as consuming cocaine, drinking excessive alcohol, etc., can improve their health by frequently visiting a religious service. Moreover, the research also found that people suffering from wrong habits can overcome them continuously.

If you observe carefully, in the above example, it is clearly visible that praying and spirituality can help overcome a person's difficulties. This is mainly because when you practice spirituality by speaking mantras, reading texts and listening to audios, you distract your mind from the problem and focus on something which gives you positive energy. Therefore, this cut-off from life problems refreshes your mind and gives you more energy to tackle the problem.

What if your prayers get unanswered?

Praying cannot solve every disease. There are several benefits of prayers, but it has some limits to their power. Some diseases such as diabetes depression require medical attention. Therefore any person who has depression should immediately seek medical assistance.

If some of your prayers don't get satisfied if you have spiritual trust, you shouldn't lose faith in spirituality. Because sometimes if we don't get something, it is for our own good. Moreover, when you don't get something, you must think that whatever happens, happens for good, because thinking this will help you in keeping a positive mindset.

"Small daily improvements are the key to staggering long-term results." – Robin Sharma

XIX
How to Build a Habit Fast

Introduction

To become good in your life, a person needs to build new habits. According to the research at Duke University, habits account for about 40 percent of our behaviors on any day. A person can ensure health, happiness, and life in general with good habits. However, there is plenty of information, and most of the information is easy to digest. Therefore for adopting a new habit, you must break down the essential things into small fragments.

In this article, we will mention different ways you implement in your life to adopt a new habit in your life.

Begin with an incredibly small habit

Most people struggle to build new habits, and they think they lack the motivation to adopt the habit. However, this is the wrong approach. Researches show that willpower is similar to a muscle. Thus similar to a muscle, willpower also gets fatigued as it gets used through the day.

Moreover, many people also think they don't have the motivation to adapt to learn new skills. Therefore, the people who think they don't have the necessary motivation should start by choosing a small habit. You don't require any motivation to do it. For instance, if you cannot do 50 pushups a day, you should begin by doing 5 pushups a day. This will help you in achieving the final target eventually.

Increase your habits in small quantities

According to Jim Rohn, success is a few disciplines practiced every day: while failure is simply a few errors in judgment, repeated every day.

If one percent improvement adds up fast, so the one percent decline. Hence, rather than trying to do something extraordinary initially, a person should start small and slowly improve. Because when you start small, then along the way, your willpower and motivation also improve. Thus with time, sticking to a habit becomes easier.

While building up, break the habits into fragments.

When you start adding small fragments to a new skill, there are chances of improving tremendously within two to three months. However, maintaining consistency is extremely important when breaking the task into small fragments. Because if you become inconsistent in learning, then there are chances that you start lagging in achieving your target.

For instance, if you want to start meditation, you must begin your journey by meditating for a few minutes a day. If you become regular with meditation for a few minutes, going long on duration with meditation can be easy. Because you will know the procedure to make that happen.

When you get to deviate from the schedule, can

come back in it

Since habit-building takes a lot of time, there are chances that you might fall off the routine during the journey. Therefore, in such a scenario, you must have the ability to come back into a routine. Because if you don't, then all the hard work you did initially will go in vain.

For example:- if you are working out every day and have been continuing with the routine for months. Due to some emergency, you left the routine for 15 days, then you must strive to get back into a routine. Because if you don't, then the hard work and dedication you have put in for getting fit will eventually fade away. Thus, it is essential for you to preserve all the hard work you have done so that you can keep on building ahead from where you left.

Moreover, when learning a habit, you shouldn't expect to fail. Instead, you should plan for failure and prepare for the worst situation. To assess the worst-case scenario, you must hold yourself and think about the situations which can lead you into worst-case scenarios. You must focus on answering the questions, such as the things which might get in your way? The daily emergencies which can prevent you from doing your habit? And how can you plan to work around these issues?

Patience is a key in habit building.

A person who has started a new skill journey should learn to be patient because the results don't come in within a few days. To get positive results, you need to be consistent and patient.

Suppose you increase weight in the gym. You must go slower than you think. Moreover, suppose you increase sales calls in your business strategy. In that case, you should start by adding fewer calls than you expected to handle.

The idea behind going slow and patiently is that the new habits should feel easy at the start. Because if you stay consistent and continue doing the habit on a regular basis, the growth will be long-lasting. Because the time you would have spent on the habit will be more. Therefore, you will have proper knowledge about it.

XX

How to Forget an Unwanted Memory

Everyone has something they want to forget. It could be an unpleasant experience, something troubling, or something you wish never took place. You know you cannot do anything to prevent the event from occurring at that moment, and the only way you can actually live not knowing about it is through forgetting. There is a difference in the memories you choose to reflect on to better yourself and memories that cause you pain.

It is better to forget something that causes you heartache and that doesn't really teach you anything. Forgetting doesn't give you sadness, instead, it gives you hope and calm to carry on about your life and have peace of mind. Psychologically there are many ways you can train yourself to forget certain events and erase them from your mind completely.

You can deliberately decide not to think about the unwanted memory at all. If you are reminded of it, either in your mind or externally, then try not to think about it. Do not let your mind wander there and avoid making that connection by going blank. Forget everything that is remotely associated with that memory. Whether it is something you can see, hear, smell, or feel, disassociate yourself from them or they might trigger your subconscious efforts.

Avoid places, object or even people who have left a bad impression on you. Push all the details related to that event out of your mind, no matter how difficult or even impossible you might think it to be. There has even been research conducted that even words that you heard during that particular event can be harmful to you. You have to forget what they had said to you if you want to completely start forgetting. Get rid of anything lying around you or in your possession that reminds you of the event.

It could be anything from photographs to letters to gifts or items left behind. Even a song can have a bad effect on you if you had already associated it with that particular memory. The only way you can get rid of that is to delete it. It is challenging initially to block out such unwanted memories, but without actively and persistently doing this, you will not be able to achieve what you wanted. You have to consciously work hard into blocking that memory from entering your thoughts. You have to practice this on a regular basis, or you will risk having it all come crashing back at you. But even the difficulty of blocking the thought can rebind on you if you give it too much importance. Keep a conscious effort that you have to remove that memory, but no to the point that it makes you unhappy or stressed when you are not able to achieve that.

Accept the fact that it is a difficult journey for you and that you need to practice as much as you can to avoid said memory. If all else fails, distract yourself by thinking about something good. Replace a bad memory with a good one instead. For example, if you have a memory of facing failure that lets you down, think about all the times you have actually succeeded. Substitute the good memory for the bad instead. Thinking about happier thoughts would keep you more preoccupied, and giving you fewer chances to think about the bad memories. You can also associate something good or positive with your bad memory.

Take your unwanted thought and associate it while doing something you love, like going for a walk or watching a movie. If you connect something positive with the negative, you will stick more to the positive note. This can also give you something called the bittersweet thought, where the unpleasantness of the unwanted thought tones down to something that gives you joy. If all this doesn't really help you, acknowledge the negative thought. If you acknowledge the bad memory and the feelings associated with it, you will be able to act on it better. Whatever you felt at that moment, amplify it.

If it was fear, hurt or sadness, feeling those emotions in your safe space can diminish that effect on you. You can also write down what you felt with that memory. Writing down your feelings will help you compose yourself better. Do not think about anything else but what you have in your mind. Once you are done, you can get rid of it by burning the paper, tearing it or shredding it. It gives you a sense that whatever you had seen, thought and felt is now erased. This is a sort of unorthodox, ritualistic approach, but may help you bring some calm to your mind. Do not think about your past. Rather focus on the present and practice mindfulness. Do not go about your day absentmindedly. Be aware of your surroundings, take in new information, and keep yourself occupied in your day to day activities. Meditation can also help you stay mindful and live in the moment.

If you can't get rid of your unwanted memories, create new happy ones instead. Keep yourself busy with new things to and new people to meet. Spend time with people you trust and love. Go on a vacation to release your tension or get socializing. Take up a new sport or activity or try something you have never done before. Keep yourself active and fit. The more time you spend on things that you love, the less time you will spend on thinking about the bad memories.

You can also try talking about it with someone you trust. It could be your closest friends or family, anyone you know will listen to you. Explain it to them what is bothering you and how you are not able to get rid of the unwanted thought no matter how much you have tried. Listen to their advice or similar stories that they would like to share with you. Maybe their perspective on it can change your views as well, making you forget the bad memory. These are just some of the many ways you can adapt in yourself to help you lead a happier, healthier life.

XXI

How to improve your memory power after the age of 60

It is scientifically proven that the older you get, portions of your brain cells that are related to memory and recollection will eventually start dying off. This, in turn, leads to old age Alzheimer or partial memory loss. If genetics are involved, then there isn't much one can do about it. But with specific diet and lifestyle changes earlier on, it has been proven to jog the memory and keep your brain activity from dying out completely. The more active you keep your mind, the fewer chances there is of you slipping into a loss of memory.

Eat a Balanced Diet:

We have been taught to eat a healthy balanced diet since we were young, but because of lack of time and societal and work pressure can put a strain on our eating habits. Skip the junk and keep a healthy appetite to gain the most for your health.

Take supplements:

Sometimes you won't get everything from your food. In that case, added nutrients and minerals are highly beneficial. To start a supplement, you need professional consultation first to find out what supplement will best suit you. Make sure you get a lot of B Vitamins since they will directly impact your brain activity and repair brain tissue.

Go for a walk:

A simple 30 minute walk every day highly beneficial for your overall health. It just does not only keep arthritis away but gives you physical energy and keeps you mentally sound. Any physical activity triggers the release of a protein called BDNF that promotes healthy nerve cells in the brain. This could lead to a boost to your memory.

Stock up on vegetables:

Avoid having artery clogging high-fat food. Keep your diet as low fat and high fiber as possible to avoid having clogged veins and arteries and, in turn, keeping the blood flowing all over your body, especially to your brain.

Reduce or avoid added sugars:

It has been scientifically proven through various research data that people who regularly consume high sugar diets have lower brain volumes and poorer memories than those who consume less sugar.

Practice meditation:

Keeping your mind stress free will lead to healthier brain growth. Meditating every day is relaxing and soothing, and has been found to reduce stress and pain, lower blood pressure, increase grey matter in the brain and improve spatial working memory.

Engage Your Brain

Just like physical exercise, mental exercise is also good for you. Join a book club, take up reading, start writing, play cards, watch sports with friends, or play a brain-training app, solve puzzles, any mentally challenging activity will keep your mind sharp even in your later ages.

Stay Socially Active:

Any social interaction helps in increased brain activity. Be it going out with friends or even a friendly chat with your neighbor, the number of friends and acquaintances someone has, the better they are at preserving mental function and memory. It also eradicates social isolation which in turn causes depression and leads to dementia.

Get Proper Sleep:

Because of lack of sleep or erratic sleep schedule, attention and concentration go down, and brain power is not as strong as it is in those who have a healthy, restful sleep. Studies have always associated sufficient sleep with better memory performance. Sleep helps combine memories.

Here are some tips to try to get better sleep:

- Avoid having big meals before bed.

- Going to sleep at the same time every day and get up at the same time each morning.

- Don't drink alcohol or anything with caffeine close to bedtime.

- Avoid smoking.

Keep Studying:

The more you take up something to learn the better mental functioning in old age. Research shows that modern style of education helps you in retention of your memory by actively switching your mental states. Solving riddles, puzzles and trying out other mental exercise is believed to help maintain individual brain cells and stimulate communication among them.

Believe in yourself:

Studies show that middle-aged and older learners don't fare so well in tasks when they're exposed to negative pre-define parameters about aging and memory, and better when the messages are showing the right results about memory preservation into old age. Older people who believe that they cannot control their mental strength fall steadily and are more likely to prone to get memory loss.

Practicing Mindfulness:

Studies have shown that being mindful lowers stress and improved concentration and memory. Mindfulness is a state of mind in which you need to focus on your present situation and maintain awareness of your surroundings and feelings. Mindfulness and meditation get along very well with each other, but the two aren't the same. Meditation is a formal practice, whereas mindfulness is a mental habit you can teach in any situation.

Repeat what you want to remember:

If you're going to recollect something you've just heard, read, or thought about, repeat it out loud or write it down. That way, you get to think about and reinforce the memory or connection. If your belonging is not there on it usual spot, tell yourself out loud what you've done. Don't hesitate to ask the concerned person to repeat the information if you were not able to catch it the first time.

Get Yourself Checked:

Certain medical conditions such as depression diabetes thyroid disease and vitamin deficiency can cause memory loss. Sometimes, certain medicines, such as sleep and anxiety pills, can also affect your ability to remember. See your doctor to get properly checked and treated for these problems and to go over all your medicines.

Take help of Memory Tricks:

When you have trouble with remembering things every day, it helps to have a few tricks up your sleeve. Every time you learn something new, maybe a new name or word, say it out loud several times to seal it in your brain. Mentally try to connect each new name with an image. To help with the recollection of relevant information such as dates and appointments, post sticky notes around the home refrigerator and office desk or use reminder applications on your phone so you'll know when it is time to take your medication or head to a crucial meeting.

I am hoping that these tips will keep your memory and brain active even at old age.

XXII

How to sharpen your observation skills

Most of you have watched this amazing TV series, Sherlock Holmes. If not, then I strongly recommend to just binge watch it on Netflix. What makes Sherlock Holmes a great detective? His observation and analyzing skills. His observation skills are out of the world. He can smell the grease off your clothes, he can notice the odd behavior of a person and can analyze the expressions and body language of anyone which eventually helps in the detective work.

Observation is simply being aware of one's surrounding. It is the acquisition of some information from a source. In scientific terms, it means recording the data of the experiments involving the use of instruments. Observation can either be qualitative or quantitative. If there is some number attached to the observed thing, then it becomes quantitative but if only the presence and absence is noted then it is qualitative.

Humans can observe a phenomenon using their 5 senses namely touch, taste, smell, hear, and sight. A strong observer uses all these 5 senses actively for observing and analyzing the surrounding. They also use their memory to make their observation skills much better because it helps in analyzing things and if they come across anything that they have already seen they can easily recall it which makes things easier.

So basically to sharpen the observation skills you need to sharpen your 5 senses and improvise your memory. Good observation skills help you in your daily life a lot, it will be helpful while studying as you can observe the pattern of solving and it is almost all the household works. You might have heard that meditation can help to enhance your observation skill, its true but there are some other things that are also required in order to improve your observation skills.

Increase your awareness

At any point in time, there are lots of thing going on in your surrounding. You hear many sounds but you don't pay attention to any of them. So try paying attention to them. Just stop wherever you are and look around, it's a wonderful world around you. Hear all the sounds, look at everything that surrounds you, the animals, the people, the plants. Feel the air and smell the surroundings. Try to acknowledge every detail of surrounding. You can also try this in every place you go, it is also advised to practice it more by going to different places.

All the big objects and big details are easy to observe but paying attention to the little details will make you a good observer, for example, seeing a phone is someone's hand is a big detail but observing what phone it is and checking out the sticker behind the phone is a quality of a good observer.

Above things seem easy but when you are surrounded by lots of distractions like smartphones, internet, television etc it becomes very difficult to just be present at the moment. You can just take these distractions out of the picture. Just go out for a walk without your phone and observe!!

You should try to make your observation quantitative whenever it's possible. Like when you are walking in a park instead of observing that there are some people sitting on the bench try to identify them as there are five people sitting on the bench.

Improving your memory

When you see something and you can quickly tell some details about that particular thing then that is considered a good observation. Because what's the point in observing something and forgetting right away. for example, when you see a phone and it has an apple engraved on its back then you quickly remember that it's an iPhone. You can also tell many of its a feature because you have already come across this device and you remember about it, so good observation indeed.

But you can't remember everything. Because every human being has different limits of memory. But you can improve it. You can train your brain to remember more things this can be done by playing games like a brain teaser. You can also create an image of that scenario which you can remember easily. Try to look for patterns because many things are related in a way so if you identify the pattern then you just have to remember the pattern only. Physical exercise also helps in improving memory because physical exercises cause more activity in our brain which helps in increasing the memory.

Sharpen your senses

This is an obvious one, you can improve the results by improving the instruments. So sharpen your senses and engage them more and get good observations. So how do you improve something- by practicing it and using it more often. Listen to every sound around you and try to identify the source of the sound it will improve your hearing senses. Identify every smell from the surrounding or the object and try to remember it so that next time you can identify the object just by smelling it.

Try to touch many objects with your eyes closed it will help you get the sense of different shape and it will sharpen your touch sense. You can sharpen your sense of taste by eating slowly and try to identify the different spices and ingredient of the food. Meditation also helps in improving your senses. Practicing mindful meditation daily will help you increase your attention and you can focus on your senses with ease. So sit quietly and comfortably and focus on your senses and identify what is around you using each one of them.

Having good observation skills will help you greatly in your life. It is beneficial everywhere and to everyone. A good observer can also analyze the mood and mind-set of other people which can help in building good relationships. It also helps in academics as many subjects have patterns which are waiting to be observed and solved. So practice the above things daily because who knows you might be the next Sherlock Holmes in the town.

**"The only way to achieve the impossible is to believe it is possible." –
Charles Kingsleigh**

XXIII
How Yoga Helps to Fight Depression

A lot of studies have been conducted in order to establish a relationship between yoga and depression. According to a recent study conducted by Harvard mental health department, yoga has the ability to subside the impact of stress. It can subsequently help with anxiety and depression issues as well. Yoga can be a technique that comes at par with meditation, relaxation, and exercise along with boosting overall energy of the body and mind. It can be explained as a physical form of exercise which entails different poses, meditation and breathing techniques.

This therapy can help tackle depression and other symptoms like problems with concentrating and energy deprivation. Several people use yoga as a medium to manage emotional and mental issues like anxiety, stress or depression, chronic conditions like back pain or long term pain in other areas and the health and wellbeing in general. Classes for this practice are available at various places like hospitals, fitness centers as well as local community centers. They can vary in intensity as per the style of yoga.

How does this therapy work and what does it provide?

Yoga therapy can be an extremely powerful weapon to kill depression. Even if yoga isn't particularly a person's thing, a combination of the physical maneuvering and meditation goes a long way because it provides two crucial factors for beating depression. Meditation holds the potential to draw a person back to the present and clear their mind off of negative emotions. The controlled movements will also help develop a strong connection between the mind and body.

According to a study, breathing techniques help to subside the symptoms of depression. Yoga may be useful if practiced because it focuses on deep, controlled breathing. It helps in:

Improvement of mood along with relaxation: yoga is a natural remedy for raising serotonin production when taken up as an exercise. According to the Psychiatry and neuroscience journal, serotonin plays a significant role in aiding depression. It boasts a person's happiness levels. A study also says that people who suffer from depression are likely to have lower serotonin levels. Yoga is essentially helpful for its calming, fluid and gentle nature in general. Every pose entailing this practice is flexible enough for people of all kinds. A typical instructor of yoga will emphasize the importance of concentration, breathing, and fluid movement. They will ask you to narrow your attention towards positive images as well in order to relive your body and mind off stress.

Reduction of stress and anxiety: yoga is known to increase a human's variation in time between heartbeats, also known as heart rate variability. It does so by raising the response to relaxation over the response to stress in the body. A high HRV translates into a good level of self – monitoring or adapting to stress in a specific manner. The practice of yoga can help decrease resting heart rate, reduce blood pressure, ease breathing process and raise the pain tolerance capability of a person because, for a fact, people with high-stress levels have a low tolerance for pain.

What are the different styles of yoga one can practice?

There are varied styles of yoga apart from the basic ones like standing forward and bending. All these styles have a different speed and approach. You can explore all of them thoroughly and select the one that works for you the best. A brief description of some styles of yoga:

Hatha: this form involves movements paced at a rather moderate rate. It is very well suited for amateurs.

Bikram: this style is supposed to be practiced in a warm room where a set series of moves will allow your blood to flow.

Vinyasa: this form develops a link between breathing and movement wherein the pace goes from low to high.

Hot: it is also placed in a warm room, but there are no fixed poses

Kundalini: this style brings together repetitive exercises which demand intense breathing

Ashtanga: this is a physically draining style which focuses on rapid and sentenced poses

Yin: this form focuses upon the elasticity and length of your muscles via back and seated poses

Iyengar: in this practice, you will have to use chairs, block or straps in order to find proper alignment in your body

Restorative: in this, the person has to move gradually through five to six poses to make him feel more at ease.

All these styles are generally taught by professional instructors, and you will be able to find them in nearby fitness studious or yoga studios. However, if you are someone who likes more of a private setting, you can go for a personal instructor or follow YouTube videos at home.

XXIV

Mental Exercises for Optimum Fitness Levels

There are plenty of physical exercises and their benefits documented accurately across the world. There are several benefits of exercising daily right from keeping your blood pressure in check to keeping heart diseases and other problems at bay. It has also been noted that physical exercises keep the physical appearance also bright and neat. With time, the benefits of physical exercises have been focused on the mental health and state, i.e. several exercises lift mood and improve sleep by reducing stress and anxiety. Along with a healthy heart and functioning joints, keeping your mind calm and focusing on your emotional wellbeing is also essential.

In this blog, we will be talking about exercises that are centered around the mind and mental health so that by focusing on them you can reach the optimum fitness level and become a high performer. The phrase 'use it or lose it' applies to the brain functioning very effortlessly.

What is brain training?

Brain training includes mental exercises which focus on the mind and functioning of the brain. In addition to that, mental exercises if performed correctly have also boosted intelligence and emotional wellbeing among people. There are several brain exercises that you could perform from time to time to keep your brain sharp and working efficiently.

Mental or brain exercises to keep your fitness at an optimum level

We are mentioning below some of the most effective yet easy brain and mental exercises which you could take up so that you can focus better on work and remain calm. The below exercises are very common among people and can be performed by the majority of people irrespective of age. Right from jigsaw puzzles to taking a stroll in the garden, you could perform these activities easily.

Solving jigsaw puzzles

Regardless of how big your jigsaw puzzle is, it strengthens your brain. It creates several cognitive abilities and prevents visuospatial cognitive aging. It challenges the brain and makes it work till you can fit the missing pieces of the puzzles.

Card games

If you don't remember the last time you played cards, then it is time for you to shuffle those decks of cards. Playing card games increases the brain volume in several brain regions and also increases memory and thinking skills. You could give solitaire, hearts, poker, crazy eights, and even rummy a shot. Card games not only sharpen your cognitive skills but also enhance your retention power.

Building up your vocabulary

One of the best ways to become smart and enhance your brain functions is through improvising on your vocabulary. Quick vocabulary sessions can get converted into brain stimulation sessions very easily. All you have to do is keep a notebook and go through different new words. Look up their meanings on the internet or in the dictionary and try using that word in your daily conversations. Vocabulary building is known to boost auditory and visual processing.

Learning a new skill

To strengthen the connections of your brain, you could take up a new skill. New skills are not only fun and interesting to learn and develop but also keep our brains hot and running. Studies have shown that new skill development contributes to the enhancement of memory function in the brain. You could take up new skills to not only kill time but also help your brain function strengthen.

Listening to music and dancing your heart out

Studies have shown that listening to music not only boosts mood but also enhances brain potential and creative thinking of the same. It is one of the easiest ways to enhance your brainpower. You can also take up learning new instruments and develop not only your skills but also increase your memory power.

In addition to that, dancing improves the memory and speed of the brain. You could take up dance classes of any form. It could not only help you in developing a skill but also allow you to have a better mood and brain functioning.

Meditation

Taking time out to meditate not only calms your body but also slows your breathing and brings peace to your mind. It has been seen that taking time out to meditate regularly makes your brain work smoothly and calmly. It fine-tunes the memory and also increases brain stability. All you have to do is find a quiet spot, sit down properly, close your eyes, and then spend time introspecting or just putting attention on one spot.

Now that you are aware of the mental exercises which will help your body to relax, you will be able to reach your fitness goal with ease. Focus on keeping your brain alert, memory retained and mind strengthened and calmed so that you can focus on the other factors that will ensure that your body is reaching the optimum fitness levels.

"What we fear of doing most is usually what we most need to do." – Ralph Waldo Emerson

XXV

10 Quick Exercises For the Brain for Busy People to Stay Mentally Fit

Sometimes one has to experience the fall if they are willing to rise because that's how they will know about the outcome if they fail. If lives of people from early Stone Age is to be considered to this 21st-century one will notice a big difference, people in that age had no wanting for example if they felt hunger they hunted, if they felt cold they rubbed stones to produce fire. They did not work for extra because they didn't know anything about extra but now just see where the humans have taken themselves. The hunger for wanting more grows up, and in all this mess the brains get affected the most.

During this process the body releases chemicals which is eventually bad for the body & at this time the brain acts more faster which will require more blood so to pump more blood the heart will need to work fast & one knows the result so why go through all this instead why not do something which will keep the brain fit. There are many exercises which will help one in keeping their brain mentally fit. Below are some of the exercises which are quick and doesn't require so much time-

- Reading- One might think that reading means reading those philosophical novels whose meaning are out of the box with containing over the top contents. It's not about that reading means reading anything until it invests you in it. Reading newspapers, articles, books, etc can be considered because reading is what boosts up one's imagination and that will require the brain to work which will eventually lead in being mentally fit. For starters read just daily newspaper and when just starts gets investing in them they can choose over other mediums too.

- Doing things in their way- Sometimes not following the universal path towards a simple thing can lead the brain to think and work. So every time just take another route to anything out there try something new, and this will surely lead the brain to work and keep it mentally fit. By this way, the brain will be forced to think and work.

• Get to the real work- As stated in a study that humans only use some fraction of their brain towards any problems or things. What if someone identifies its full capacity and then use it. It is not a difficult task one just has to get themselves in the situation where they have to use all of their senses towards anything and then see how things turn out for them.

• One should challenge themselves- If one is finding it difficult to challenge them ten challenges the individual in the mirror. Make betas or keep a reward so that the work should be done with efficiency. The reward can be anything it doesn't have to be a cup or a prize; it can be anything.

• Wander out and get connected with people- Sometimes when one cut themselves off with the world leads to unstable mental conditions. So a simple way to get things on the right path is to go out there and connect with people. Connecting with others opens up the gate of new ideas and trick about how to live life more freely. An individual sometimes finds this solution a hard one because they find difficulty in connecting. But a simple start will ease out the work.

• Meditation- This is the most important techniques because this isn't just some exercise it a way to open up the mind to a different world. It helps people being motivated and energized. This should not be seen as an exercise instead one should make this as part of their life so coping up with the meditation would be easy.

• Exercising- Physical exercise helps in maintaining good mental strength. By exercising the body is stress-free and then the tension loosens up as the muscles of the body get into the real work. Starting the morning with some exercises with keeping the individual boosted for the day which will eventually lead into a good mental strength.

• Buckling up for creative things- Doing just those old fashioned things or following the order routine might slow the brain down. So why not change the things and replace them with creative stuff.

• Switch the main hand- If one is right handed then tray to do the same things with the left hand. As this will change everything and will force the brain to work and think.

• Take the help of technology- This is the thing which is responsible for this state of mind because it was used in a bad way. So why not use it for good deeds like planning out things with mobile applications or tracking the exercises etc.

XXVI

Positive Influence of Gratitude in Success

Introduction

When we desire to achieve something, we quickly switch to science. When we are struggling, we think about taking a pill that can get us through the struggle and take us to success straightaway. Moreover, many of us start looking outside for things that make us feel better, give us more self-esteem, etc. While searching for these things, we forget the basic principle of life, which is gratitude.

Many researches have been conducted in the past. All of them have indicated that having an attitude of gratitude can help you reap big benefits. A person who is thankful for everything from work, health, family to being alive is actually on the right path for achieving success.

On the contrary, a person who approaches life with a negative mindset will approach success and failure completely differently. A person who addresses life with a negative attitude won't enjoy their work and will find it difficult to cope with the failures they will face. In this article, we will mention the benefits of an attitude of gratitude.

Celebrate smallest things

For being grateful, you don't need to be a superhuman. All you need to do is observe your life and think about the different things you should be grateful for. Because in our life, there are many things which get unnoticed. Such as a new pair of branded shoes, fancy clothes, costly gadgets, expensive food, etc. These are some of the things which gets unnoticed when a person isn't grateful. We don't recognize these things in life as an achievement, and that's why we ignore their importance. Thus celebrating the little achievements you have received will help you stay positive and motivated towards achieving your goal.

Don't feel afraid while saying 'thank you.'

To adopt the attitude of gratitude, you can begin by greeting people around you. Because when you achieve something in life, it is not only because of your hard work, but it is also due to the people around you who have motivated and supported you at different stages of the process. Moreover, saying 'thank you to someone makes them feel that you value their efforts and mean something to you. Moreover, when you say 'thank you to someone, it lifts their mood and makes them feel better.

Always reply to the person who has helped you.

Today, people are extremely busy in their lives. Everyone today is just sitting in front of their laptops and thinking about completing their targets. However, it is important for a person to hold themselves up and think about their well-wishers. Thus, even in the middle of chaos, a person should wait and think about the things for which they should be grateful. The things can even be small. Such as a person who gave their phone to you to make a phone call when your phone is dead. Thus, appreciating such small moments in life will help you generate positive vibes, which is important for a healthy mind.

Create a Gratitude journal

Writing things down is the most powerful way to remember what you have achieved in life. Journaling helps you in figuring out your deepest thoughts and desires. Moreover, when you are inclined to give gratitude, journaling can be a brilliant way to figure out the beauty of life. You should designate a stipulated amount of time each day for starting journaling. If you become consistent at it, then steadily you will come to know about its benefits.

Gratitude makes a person happy.

A famous personality was asked whether happiness is directly linked to being grateful? In reply, the person said that generosity is the only creator of happiness in this world. He gave examples of people who have been through turmoil and bad days. Still, they chose to stay humble and graceful even when losing their temper was the easier option. He added that these people are a great example of generating happiness through gratitude.

Gratitude enhances self-esteem

Several researches have been conducted, and they have shown that gratitude has made people kinder and friendlier. Thus grateful people have more social capital. A person who is grateful to others has a higher chance of getting help from others. Moreover, gratitude increases the recognition of generosity. For example, a person with low self-esteem observes a person helping others think that the helper is actually helping others thinking about favor in return. However, a grateful person will consider it as an act of kindness.

Gratitude can be a great energy booster because a person who is grateful will always feel good about themselves. Thus a person who always thinks of doing well to others will always be feeling good. Moreover, if the gracious person combines their gratitude with positive mantras, then it will increase your confidence as well.

XXVII
Self Help Tips to Fight Depression

1. Get in a routine

If you are feeling depressed, you need to get into a routine. Depression can strip away and break down the structure of your life. For one day, try to adhere to a routine, and you will feel inclined to follow it the next day too. Setting a gentle but firm daily schedule can help you get back on track.

2. Set goals

When you're depressed, you can feel like you cannot achieve any goal. That can make you feel worse about yourself. To push back the depression, set daily goals for yourself. Start very small and make your goal something that you can succeed at, even if it is a small thing like doing the dishes every other day. As you begin to feel better, you can add more challenging daily life goals.

3. Exercise

Exercise temporarily boosts the feel-good chemicals in your brain called endorphins. It also has long term advantages for people with depression. Regular exercise encourages the brain to rewire itself in positive ways and focus on the brighter aspects of life. That does not mean you have to run marathons to get benefitted from the exercise. Just walking a few miles every day can help.

4. Eat healthily

Although there is no magic diet that can fix depression, it is a good idea to watch what you eat. If depression has a habit of making you overeat, being in control of your eating habits will help you feel better. Although nothing is definitive, there is enough evidence that foods with omega-3 fatty acids like salmon and tuna and folic acid-containing vegetables like spinach and avocado can help ease depression.

5. Get enough sleep

Depression can make it hard to get enough sleep, and a lack of sleep can make your depression symptoms worse. You can avoid this by making some changes to your lifestyle. Go to bed and switch off the lights every day. Also, remember to get up at the same time every day. Try not to nap between the waking hours or any work that you are doing. Take all the distractions out of your bedroom, even if it is something entertaining like a computer or TV. In the meantime, you will find that your sleep has improved.

6. Take on responsibilities

When you're depressed, you may want to pull back or retract from life and give up your responsibilities both at home and at work. Do not do that, no matter how disinterested you are. Staying involved and having your daily share of responsibilities can help you maintain a lifestyle that can counter depression. Work and any responsibility will ground you and give you a sense of accomplishment. It's okay if you are not up to full-time school or work. Think about the part-time jobs that you can do like volunteer work.

7. Challenge negative thoughts

Your fight against depression involves a lot of the work, which is mental and can change how you think. When you are depressed, you mostly jump to the worst possible conclusions that you can imagine. The next time you are feeling terrible about yourself, use logic as a natural treatment against depression. You might feel like no one likes you, but convince yourself that there is no solid evidence for that. You might feel like the most worthless person on the planet, but then make a list of people to whom you are indispensable. True, it takes practice, but with the time you can beat back those negative thoughts.

8. Check with your doctor before using supplements

There is promising evidence that certain supplements can bring about depression. These supplements include fish oil, folic acid, and SAMe. Although more research needs to be done before we can know for sure, it is wise to check with a doctor before taking any supplement.

9. Do something new

When you're depressed, you're in a nasty pothole. To get yourself up from there, push yourself to do something different like volunteering at a soup kitchen or taking a language class. When we challenge ourselves to do something new and different, there are chemical changes triggered in the brain. Trying something new alters the levels of dopamine, a brain chemical which is associated with pleasure, enjoyment, and learning.

10. Try to have fun

If you are depressed, make time to do things you enjoy. When nothing seems fun anymore, you are just plunging yourself in the pit of depression.

Although it may sound strange, you must put effort at having fun. Plan things you used to enjoy previously, even if they feel uninteresting now. Keep going to the movies or having dinner with your friends. When you are depressed, you can lose the will to enjoying life. To combat depression, you have to relearn how to have fun again.

XXVIII
Top 10 Self-help Tips to fight Anxiety

Another one of the major problems, and issues faced by a wide number of people, especially teenagers and college students, is anxiety. Anxiety is a symptom, you can say, or maybe an indicator of an underlying medical condition or a disease. Anxiety is a very normal and very healthy emotion, but when it becomes excessive and when it becomes severe and uncontrollable, it soon turns into a medical condition that can give birth to even more serious problems like depression, or ADHD or OCD.

What is Anxiety?

Anxiety is basically when a person becomes overwhelmed with worry, doubts, and extensively, intensely, and very persistently overthinks everything. This emotion is embedded in every human, and it's very common to come out in times when it's supposed to like, before public speaking, or before playing an instrument or singing in public. But when this emotion becomes a condition medically and promises to consume you every day, that is when it starts becoming a serious problem.

Some problems and some physical or internal discomfort that might happen are, the heart rate can go up by a lot, you might start sweating, and feeling restless and fidgeting with everything around you and you might feel breathless and hence might start breathing rapidly. You feel anxiety about the simplest of things and something which might be very vague, but that is when you need to understand that it is seriously affecting the life of the person, and it should be solved.

Tips to take care of the condition – Anxiety might be as serious as it might consume you when it becomes as regular and as consistent. So to stop that from happening, it needs to control, and it needs to be contained. Below are some tips that might help you deal with anxiety and get rid of the condition:

Stay Active: Whenever you feel that anxiety is about to hit you, try to divert your mind into more active things. Exercising is one such thing. Staying fit and exercising daily will make you feel good about yourself and will prevent the worry or the distraction from the condition. It also will help you keep yourself healthy, fit, and in check.

Sleep: Sleep is one of the most important medicines that help you heal, and that helps you relax in times of need. Stressed individuals need at least 8 hours of sleep every day. Less sleep will make you tiresome and will make you worry more and make you feel stressed and low.

Reduce consumption of caffeine or alcohol: Caffeine is an upper, and alcohol is a downer, and both of them can induce panic attack and hyperactivity and induce anxiety. You should cut back and prevent yourself from having them whenever you can. Drink water instead. It will help.

Positivity: Positivity is by far the most important thing you need to take care when you are prone to befall anxiety as a condition. Whenever something negative happens, remember there is always something positive that came out of it. Remove negative thoughts from your brain and always induce positivity in your life. It'll help you in all walks of life, forever, and helps you keep stress away.

Acceptance: You need to learn to accept everything. And by acceptance, I don't mean anything wrong. I mean that whatever happens is for good. Remember that and always accept any outcome that comes your way. You cannot ever control everything that you wish to. You need to accept that, and that will help you de-stress yourself and keep your anxiety in check.

Know about your worries: You need to be your solution. You need to learn and understand the things that make you worry and stress all the time. You need to find out the things that make you overthink the most. You can write in a journal, find a pattern, and find solutions to it. This will help you worry less and also, along with it; consistent anxiety won't be a problem anymore.

Deep Breathing: Deep breathes are the body's way of telling the brain that you are okay. So whenever you get much stressed, or you are worrying or excessively thinking about something, take deep breathes, and keep yourself calm and collected. That way, you know you can keep yourself in control while thinking about the solution to the problem as well.

Talk: Talking to your close friends and loved ones always help. Whenever you feel overwhelmed or out of place or stressed about something, telling them would ease the condition a lot. You can even talk to a professional like a therapist who can help you out with it.

Me time: You always need to chalk out some time for yourself. You need to take a time out from all stress and problems and do something more refreshing like listening to music to clear your head.

Balanced meals: Diet is also an important factor in making yourself feel healthy, and a well-balanced diet helps you boost your energy while keeping you fit and keeping your health in check.

XXIX

10 Most Intelligent People of High IQ of Our Times

The fact that the most intelligent person uses a mere fifteen percent of his brain is astoundingly jaw-dropping. These people send shockwaves into the world and to see what they are capable of is surreal. But if we think ahead of it and try wondering about a person who has used about thirty percent of his brain, how much frenzy would it cause in your nerve system? The people mentioned in the list below are highly intelligent intellectuals with god-like abilities. These are the ten most intelligent people in the world that are alive and working today:

Terence Tao: this man has an IQ that goes beyond a nursery kid's number dictionary. Yes, it's a whopping 230 in figure. Interestingly, when this man was at a tender age of two, he would teach five-year-old kids to spell and add up numbers. At the age of ten, he began indulging in mathematical Olympiads and won prestigious medals over the years that followed. He got his bachelors and masters both at sixteen years of age and Ph.D. by the time he was twenty. All these facts are absolutely insane.

Christopher Hirata: he is an American astrophysicist and cosmologist with a boast-worthy IQ of 225. When he was thirteen years old, he bagged a gold medal by winning the international physics Olympiad. At the age of sixteen he was already working at NASA for the possible operations on Mars and at the age of twenty-two he achieved his doctorate from Princeton University.

Kim Ung – Yong: this man is fifty- five years old and has brainpower exceeding the capacities of Hawking and Einstein. He has landed a position in The Guinness Book of World Records with a commendable IQ of 210. Very astonishingly, he uttered his first words when he was just about four months old and by the age of two he was able to read Japanese, English, Korean and German. He was invited by NASA itself for education in the states at a mere age of eight.

Christopher Langan: he is an autodidact from America and he is sixty-five years old. Quite famously known as the wittiest man of the states, his IQ stands between 195 and 210. The guy got a perfect score in his SAT irrespective of the fact that he slept through the entire exam. He has been instrumental in developing the Cognitive-Theoretic Model of the universe.

Rick Rosner: he is fifty – seven years old and has probably done a plethora of jobs ranging from being a bouncer, stripper, nude model and a roller skating waiter. He takes in tons of pills regularly in order to maintain his IQ level.

Garry Kasparov: he is a Russian and a chess prodigy being a world chess champion at the age of twenty – two. Currently fifty – four, he had got an IQ of 190. He holds a record of victories at professional tournaments, Oscars of chess and he also led the United civil front movement which was made to oppose Putin's policies.

Sir Andrew Wiles: he is a 64 years old English mathematician who managed to crack the Fermat's last theorem which is technically the world's one of the most difficult mathematical problems as per records. He has been rewarded well for the contributions to the stream of mathematics including the likes of Shaw prize, Mathematical union silver plaque and national academy of sciences. His IQ is at level 170.

Judit Polger: now forty – one, this lady beat Bobby Fischer (IQ level 180) at a tender age of fifteen only to become the youngest chess grandmaster. She was Hungarian by descent. In 2002, she broke records yet again by beating the world topper Garry Kasparov (IQ level 190). She is the only proud woman holder of a rank in the FIDE's list of top 100. Her IQ is 170.

Paul Allen: he is quite famously known as the co-founder of Microsoft with an IQ of 170 as well. At the age of sixty – four, he has a net worth of 17.5 billion dollars which most of us can only dream of making. He stands 51st in the richest people on the planet list. He is the proud owner of NFL team Seahawks and NBA team Portland trailblazers. He has also made generous donations of his money for the advancement of technology, wildlife conservation, science and education.

Stephen Hawking: Stephen Hawking is not at all an unknown name. now seventy – five, he has an IQ of 160 just like Einstein did. He is a theoretical physicist, author and cosmologist by profession. He suffers from an unusual form of ALS which has led to gradual paralysis of his body but he has survived quite more than expected luckily. He is extremely famous for his theories on black holes.

XXX

Leonardo Da Vinci and Building Habit of Creativity

This man was the best-known artist of the Renaissance who had a multitude of interests which included invention, architecture, sculpting, cartography and a lot of such things. He was considered to be the best painter of his time. His famous work includes Mona Lisa, The Last Supper, Salvator Mundi, etc. He was categorized as one of the greatest geniuses of his time. He was not only interested in arts but also had an aptitude for science and technology. He made great discoveries in fields like neuroanatomy and neurophysiology. He had immense curiosity and vivid imagination. He was also stupendous in sports. Some of the lessons that we can take from his creativity are:

Maintaining Curiosity and Learning Continuously

The stupendous work of this man teaches us to have unquenchable inquisitiveness about things and having a mind that is ever ready to learn. Continuously learning leads to an enlightened mind. The source of learning can be anything from books to dialogues etc. We can learn effectively from people only when we approach them like a novice. We cannot allow more information to flow into us if our cup of knowledge is already full. However, creativity does not mean that we need to have a lot of knowledge about everything. Minimal knowledge enhances creativity as we approach things in our unique way.

Being Completely Aware Of One's Senses

When one yearns for knowledge to quench his curiosity, his senses are automatically enhanced. Leonardo Da Vinci generated a myriad of masterpieces and made a lot of discoveries because of the way he viewed the world. What he perceived made him transform science and engineering in the process. This quality can be inculcated in us only when we shift our attention from what others are doing and concentrate on us and our talents. Comparison with others kills creativity and makes us restless.

Thinking And Dreaming Big Things

Thinking and dreaming big enables a person to reach beyond what is known by other people. It also involves deserting already known things. This also unlocks a plethora of possibilities for creative work and for finding out great opportunities. The way we think has a direct impact on the type of work we do. If we want to attract better things in our life, we need to start by working on our paradigm.

Being Aware Of What Is Happening Around

To create something new, one needs to be cognizant of the patterns that are present around him. Leonardo Da Vinci had a paradigm that all things have a connection. He taught people that one should have an open eye for patterns and parallels in the universe. To create new things one needs to be aware of what is the latest trend and what is happening around him and then bring changes according to his creativity.

Acknowledging the Point of Views of Others

Concentrating on a single point of view imperils our creativity. To bring out the best from our work we should be ready to communicate our ideas with others and accept valuable feedback. We should not bring our ego when it comes to learning. We should have an open mind while learning things from others. This will allow knowledge to flow into us from all directions.

Taking courageous Actions

We should not ponder about the opinions of others before presenting our ideas. Thinking too much about how people will perceive our actions and plans can thwart our actions. It is extremely beneficial to take courageous actions to portray our skills in front of others. Sharing one's knowledge will not only yield them respect but will also be extremely beneficial for others. Sharing of knowledge has a lot of benefits.

Admitting Our Faults

There is no perfection without errors. Therefore it is very important to acknowledge our errors and then rectify them accordingly. Leonardo Da Vinci made huge fiascos in his life, but his optimism attitude never allowed him to stop. He taught mankind that it is normal to commit errors. One of the most famous errors of Leonardo Da Vinci was the Last Supper painting. One should not only learn from his errors but also the errors of others.

Having a balance between mind and body

It is extremely important to have a body that is healthy to let creativity flow through the mind. A healthy body enables the mind to be sharp and be filled with ideas. Leonardo Da Vinci was also a marvelous athlete. One should engage in total body fitness that includes spiritual, mental as well as physical fitness. An absence of any one of these can lead to dissatisfaction. One should enjoy one's life to the fullest and include certain spontaneous plans.

XXXI
Intellectual Powers of Nicola Tesla

Modern society owes a lot to the Serbian American scientist Nikola Tesla. With over 300 patents under his name, traces of his inventions can be found in many modern day devices like radios and power grids. Hailed as the intellectual of his era, not all of his ideas came to fruition. Some of his ambitious dreams like wireless transmission of energy went unrealized. In other cases, what he invented was not practical enough such as the bladeless steam turbine, or they were too dangerous to be used such as a steam-powered electric generator also known as the "earthquake machine," after it supposedly caused an earthquake in New York City. At times, Tesla's ideas were too revolutionary to be fathomed. Some of his theoretical inventions, such as the "death ray" weapon and force field, exist only in science fictions till date.

However, 70+ years since Tesla's death, some of the eccentric ideas of the inventor have come to be realized with the future hope of development. Here is a look at some of the most bizarre ideas of Nicola Tesla that has some ties to reality.

The thought camera

Nicola Tesla had thought about inventing the machine to read about the images created by the human mind, a concept he called 'photographing of thought.' In 1893, while carrying out certain investigations, he was convinced that a particular image formed in thought must produce a corresponding image on the retina by reflex action. If the image can be illuminated and photographed, then using the usual methods, it can be projected on the screen.

If it could be successfully executed, then anything imagined by a person can be reflected on the screen as they are formed, and the minds of every individual can be read. Our minds can be depicted as open books. Although Tesla's plan never transformed into reality, researchers are still studying vision and exploring the idea of machines for mind reading. Scientists have created artificial retinas using sophisticated mathematical analyses to depict how retinas convert images to electrical impulses to send up to the brain. In making attempts to read minds, scientists have developed algorithms to interpret brain signals and reproduce a rough version of images.

Live streamed video

Back in the early nineties, Tesla had a rough grasping of the process of live streaming of videos like in modern-day laptops and smartphones. He predicted that by applying the principles of radio, devices in the future would allow people to see distant events, according to the Associated Press. The futuristic idea predicted that people would be able to watch the inauguration of a president, the playing of a baseball game or the havoc of an earthquake as though we were present on the spot.

Wireless electricity

Considered as the greatest ambition of Tesla, his dream was to wirelessly transmit energy across long distances using air as a medium. He demonstrated the possibility to light up lamps using the method of inductive coupling wirelessly. Although he was not successful in building a long-range system to broadcast energy, researchers today have developed several techniques to bring Tesla's dream closer to reality. From wireless charging of devices at home to power supplies for space elevators, scientists are expanding the range of use of wireless transmission. However, there are some major barriers, and working prototypes for short-range wireless transmission of electricity have a long way to go before they can be commercially used.

Contact with aliens

In 1899, Tesla spent time experimenting with high-frequency electricity and wireless telegraphy. He picked up peculiar radio signals on his instruments which he believed were of extraterrestrial origin. Tesla was familiar with electrical disturbances produced by the sun, Aurora Borealis, and earth currents and was sure that these signals were due to none of those causes. He noted that changes were taking place periodically with such number and order that they were not traceable. He believed that the signals originated from life from another planet. Although the scientific community dismissed the possibility of sighting aliens, they agreed that he might have picked up cosmic radio waves, which was undiscovered at the time. Otherwise, he may have received the radio messages that Marconi was transmitting from Europe.

Cell phones

In 1901, when working on the creation of Trans-Atlantic radio, Tesla proposed the idea of a modern-day cell phone to J.P. Morgan, his funder. His idea was to create a World Telegraphy System that allowed instant communication between individuals carrying handheld devices. Tesla believed Morgan could make money by manufacturing such devices with both transmitters and receivers. His concept of cell phones that could be used by anyone to communicate send voice messages and play music in distant places ushered a new era consumer culture that largely characterizes the 21st century.

XXXII
Thinking Habit for Positive Outcomes

If you are aware of the concept of glass half empty/ full then you might also be aware of the terms called optimism and pessimism. Both these terms and believing in either of these terms affect both your body and mental health. In addition to that, studies have also concluded that it is better to be an optimistic person or a positive thinker rather than someone who is a believer in pessimism. Positive thinking is no magic, and won't make lives easier. But it can change life slowly for the better by providing you with the energy and mood to tackle hardships and problems rationally.

What are the benefits of positive thinking?

An old study conducted between the years 2004 to 2012, proved that around 70,000 women who believe in positive thinking have lower chances of dying due to stroke, heart diseases, different types of cancer, infection, or even respiratory diseases.

In addition to the lower risks of dying from certain diseases, if you are a positive thinker then it enhances your quality of life, increases your energy levels, and helps you to achieve better mental and physical health. Along with that, it has been noted that positive thinkers have a faster and better rate of recovery from injuries and illnesses compared to negative thinkers and pessimistic people. The chances of people suffering from colds also decrease along with the rate of becoming depressed. It helps you to manage your daily schedule better and also allows you to cope with stress better. Last but not the least, positive thinking helps you to live longer.

How do come up with positive thoughts?

There are several techniques following which you can achieve positive thinking. Involving yourself in positive self-talk, focusing on the good and positive imagery being some of them. Since problems, hardships, and obstacles are part of life, you need to focus on the good every time you come across one. The key is to focus on the good when there is a challenge regardless of how small the good might be.

Gratitude- Thanking people

Practicing gratitude is another way of coming up with positive thoughts regularly. Gratitude practice is known to reduce stress, enhance self-esteem and even create resilience during difficult situations. Always remember the events, people, and moments that put a smile on your face and even provide you comfort. Thanking people and forgiving people are two essential practices that help you to increase the positivity around you.

Maintaining a journal

Always note down the things you are grateful for at the end of the day. No matter how insignificant they might be, it is always recommended to write down the things which made you smile throughout the day.

Finding out reasons to laugh

Several studies have proved that laughter reduces stress, anxiety, and depression in certain cases. It lightens the mood and improves stress management in people. Keep your mind open for laughter regardless of the situation you are in because it will make you feel less stressed even though the situation might be stressful. Instead of cursing yourself for messing it out, try approaching the situation differently. A little positive self-talk can go a long way.

Find out the areas which cause negativity in you

The key is to find the areas where you are the most negative. If you are unable to identify it yourself then you might ask your friend who can trust. You need to find an accurate insight so that you can identify the negative areas. You need to cater to one negative area at a time.

Initiate your state with a positive note

Start your day by telling yourself you are worth every day and it is okay to not have the best day every day. Make positive affirmations in the morning to ensure most of your day will pass by with a positive attitude. You can start the day by listening to positive and happy music.

Negative impacts of prolonged negative thinking

Prolonged negative thinking could increase headaches, body aches, fatigue, nausea, and even difficulty in getting proper sleep. Negative thinking triggers several areas in your body which could result in irregular hormone secretion and even hurts the metabolism. In addition to that, it could also hamper the immunity system negatively.

You cannot move your thoughts from negativity to positivity overnight. With consistent efforts and practice, with time you can build up more positive thoughts and lead your life more positively. If the negative thinking persists for long, then you could opt for medical help and seek therapy. Persistent negative thinking could impact not only your mind but also your body. With consistent positive affirmations and consistent positive thinking, both your mental and physical health will enhance and you will have higher energy levels to perform better.

XXXIII

Top Essentials Nutrients for the Proper Growth of Your Baby's Brain

As stated in a fact that if a human body started growing like a body of the baby means grows at that rate then imagines how much big one can get in some years only. In that critical stage of growing the brain needs nutrients which will eventually help your baby's body in the development. Sometimes when there is an absence of these nutrients than these results in welcoming of several unknown diseases which are incurable and will surely affect the growth of your baby's brain. So here is a list of nutrients which are considered among the top in essential nutrients for the proper growth of your baby's brain. The list is given below as follows-

• Zinc- This is used by the body to repair cells and produce energy which at last will lead to the development of the brain which is the most important thing in the body. Deficiency of zinc is traced back to the time when the baby is in the mother's womb from there onwards if zinc is deficient then it will surely affect the development of your child's brain, it can be in growth or internal organs not being fully developed. Meats, eggs, soy products are some of the major sources of the Zinc which contains this in a reserved manner.

• Iron- When the brain is in the developing stage it needs oxygen more than ever then because that is the key to the development of the brain. So what this iron does it carries the oxygen around with the help of the blood and distributes it among the whole body or the place where it is needed the most. This is the key ingredient required in the development of the baby's brain. Iron is required more by the pregnant woman than the normal women as this is also required in the womb. Fish, beans, seeds are the natural source of the iron.

• Copper- Copper acts as an antioxidant in the fetal and neonatal brain. If there is a deficiency of copper in the body of the baby, then there will be poor brain functionality which will affect the development of the brain. Organ meats, oyster. Green leafy vegetables are some of the sources which are enriched with copper.

• Iodine- Iodine which is helpful for the development of the thyroid hormones which eventually leads to the development of the brain by backing up the zinc content which is also helping in the development of the brain and that's how iodine helps. Iodine is present in table salt, eggs, and some processed foods.

• Folate- Folate is helpful in cell formation of the body, growth and helps in building the genetic material which then eventually develops the brain. Its deficiency sometimes leads to delay in development and disoriented immune function. Folate is mainly found in dark green leafy vegetables, grain bread, and grain products.

• Calcium- This is the most important nutrient which is useful for the development of the bones and teeth of the body which then provides proper communication between the body and the brain. It is known to make the structure of the body on which the body mass depends. Apart from this the calcium also develops a proper communication within the muscle and all the nerve cells. Calcium is found mainly in all the soy products and leafy vegetables. The dosage of calcium should be the same as the doctor prescribes because it is different for the different age groups.

• Magnesium- This nutrient is essential in keeping the internal organ of the body working properly as they are designed to function and this helps the brain to develop more and function properly. Magnesium is required less by the children under the age of 6 months, but after that, this is needed more than ever by the organs on the body. By maintaining the heartbeat, it keeps the nerves signaling as they are required to do and also keeps the bones healthy and the brain developed. The best sources of the magnesium are soya beans, almonds, bananas, and kiwi these sources not only contain magnesium in them but also have iron combined in them. These sources will also fulfill the requirements of vegetables and grains.

- Potassium- All the above-mentioned nutrients are required in the growing stage of the baby's brain, but after some time only potassium is the nutrient which can fulfill the requirements of the brain. The requirements of babies in their early stage are just a part of the bigger show the real deal starts when they start to grow. The potassium helps the body to keep the water level the same as required and also keeps the water level where required helping the brain to function properly. This then keeps all the function of the brain stable. This nutrient is mainly found in many fruits and vegetables but especially in the tomatoes which are known to full with potassium content.

XXXIV

8 Tips to reduce the number of thoughts from your mind

Every day we are plagued with numerous day to day thoughts. These thoughts can range from either something good to something terrible or awful. We cannot stop these thoughts from running through our mind, but we can teach ourselves to keep a calm head. With persistent practice, you can change the way you think, or even reduce the number of negative thoughts you have. Unwanted thoughts will only trigger unhappiness and dissatisfaction in your life. You can do well without these interferences. Instead, focus on bettering yourself, your life, and others around you. With the right amount of dedication, you can reduce the number of thoughts that go through your mind. Here are some steps to show you how to accomplish that.

Stop or avoid contemplation.

If something is bothering you and the solution is beyond your control, stop thinking about it. Negative thoughts will only lead to a negative outlook on life. Sometimes these thoughts just cross your mind, and you can't help thinking about it, even if you try not to. This is only natural, and there are some steps you can take to avoid that.

Imagine the extreme worst.

If you think about the worst case scenario that can ever happen, then you will have to think about how you are going to handle it. If you can think through that with a proper outcome, then you are well equipped to handle that situation, thus reducing your worry.

Keep time out for your thoughts.

Set aside some time to worry and think about your problems. If you think about it, you will be able to reach a solid conclusion and give it some thought and attention that it needs. Or on the contrary, this can also help you stop thinking about the problem excessively.

Go outside.

Go for a walk or just step outside to clear your head. Getting yourself outside will help you reduce the strain on your thoughts and might even get you preoccupied with new things that you will see, hear and smell.

Believe in yourself.

The only person who can bring about change in yourself is you alone. For that, you have to have the faith and belief that you can channel your innermost positive thoughts and shut out all the negative views. Keep a positive head and you can definitely tackle your problems. If you stay focused on the good, you can always improve. The more you keep this up, the more likely you can make the desired advances in your life than people who have a fixed and intangible mindset.

Have an optimistic approach for yourself.

If you want to control your thoughts, you have to be optimistic about it. Degrading yourself will only negatively impact you and your ability to move on from the situation. If you are overly optimistic about being able to control your thoughts and behavior, you can help give yourself more self-control over the problem. You have to convince yourself that you will succeed and that you can take control of your mind, even if you do not believe it.

Stop blaming yourself.

Some things are out of your control and you have to accept that. If you cannot change the outcome of whatever has transpired, then you should not put yourself down. Do not take personal responsibility for things that you cannot control. If you feel like you're putting yourself down, then question yourself what you could have done to change the situation if at all you were present.

Do not jump to conclusions

Think and evaluate yourself and your thoughts before reaching a conclusion. If there is no evidence to back up your claims, stop thinking about it. Do not judge too quickly and do thorough research before reaching that point.

Do not overgeneralize everything.

What you have experienced in your past does not necessarily affect your future. Overgeneralizing is taking a just one instance out of a negative experience and matching it with the expectations of your future, no matter how false it may be. You should be the change to your future, and you can only achieve that through hard work and persistence.

Stop catastrophizing on your thoughts.

Catastrophizing is blowing things out of proportion. Overthinking will lead to dire consequences and will just make you unhappy. Work on your positive thoughts instead. Question yourself and fight this off with logic and reason.

Do not stress yourself.

Your body and mind are connected to each other. If your body is stressed, you can expect your mind to be stressed as well. During stressful situations, people lack self-control. It is vital to decrease stress in your life as much as possible to protect your self-control energy. There are many ways to reduce stress, and some of them are given below.

• Relaxation techniques such as deep abdominal breathing will give you the peace you crave. You can also try focusing on a single soothing word (such as calm or peace).

• Exercising is also essential to relax your mind and muscles.

• Being social can help you get out of your shell. Spend time with friends and family to get your mind off your worries.

Research shows that spending time or money on others can bring you happiness, peace, and calmness.

If you are happy, you increase your self-image and in retrospect will also help you reduce all you're pent up negative feelings that make self-control harder to attain.

The way you plan on spending your time or money on others is not that important. What matters most is that it helps you and those around you and they take value in what you are doing for them.

If you find it hard to combat your negative feelings, all you have to do is simply smile. Smiling helps dispel all the negative feelings that reduce self-control. If your self-control is down, it becomes more difficult for you to control your mind. Smiling can actually cause you to feel happy and bring in happiness.

These are some useful tips to help you dispel random negative thoughts from your mind.

XXXV

How to Train Your Brain to Stay Calm in Emergencies

It is a common propensity of humans to be restless at times of emergency. We often are unable to make rational decisions during such times as umpteen thoughts are passing our minds. However, the types of decisions that we take during such times are mostly emotional and not rational. Therefore it is essential to calm our brain during such emergencies. The first thing to remember during a crisis is to take a deep breath as this enables oxygen to flow to our brain.

Another important thing to commemorate is to have immense faith in us and be optimistic. Optimism is the key to solve all problems. Instead of trying to seek help from others, we should try to stay calm for 5 minutes by removing all external distractions like our phones and then mentally psych ourselves to take appropriate actions as required by the situation. Some of the other steps that we should inculcate in our daily routine to stay calm during an emergency are:

Include exercise in our schedule

Physical activity keeps not only our body but also our mind healthy. It burgeons the flow of oxygen to our brain. It also helps in releasing hormones that enable the growth of the cells of the brain. Exercise helps our memory to retain information for long periods. It also reduces our stress levels and anxiety. Now it is not mandatory to join a gym and spend umpteen hours there. Even a brisk walk of 30 minutes can do good. Initially one needs to push oneself to exercise as it is easier to be a couch potato than exercise. However with consistency, one can find ecstasy in exercise.

Meditation

This technique has also been scientifically verified as one of the best techniques to relax one's mind. Meditation has a myriad of advantages to boast about. It enables us to thwart all the negative thoughts in us and just focus on our skills. Even 10 minutes of meditation before starting the day can act as a potent weapon. A lot of people are however unaware about how to do meditation properly. The correct of doing meditation is to plug in earphones and then try to listen to the sound of silence. The sound of silence is like the one which we can hear in the mountain while driving our cars. Initially, it is difficult to listen to the sound however with practice one can easily listen to this sound. Almost all successful entrepreneurs and multitaskers meditate. The practice of meditation should be inculcated as early as possible.

Inculcate organization of tasks every day

It is extremely important to organize our day to day tasks and plan out everything that has to be included in our schedule. The planning has to be done according to the priority of the tasks. We should also assign a period for specific tasks so that we can complete all tasks within a particular period. This also enables us to eradicate the tendency to panic. There is a multitude of apps available online to plan our day. Now the organization needs to be a done in a way that we can follow the plan properly. Many people tend to make a plan that is hard materialize since they include a lot of things in the task. One needs to develop a timetable according to one's comfort.

Learn to do one thing at a time

Our mind can concentrate on only one task at a time. If we try to do multiple jobs at a time, it will drive us crazy. Many of us misunderstand the concept of multitasking. Multitasking means as soon as we finish one task, we switch to another task and then completely focus on the task at hand. It is also very important to know how to relax our brain after a task is over as it will enable the brain to concentrate more on the other tasks. Music is the best way to relax oneself. There are so many genres of music to choose from depending upon one's mood.

Know how to motivate oneself

We cannot rely on external sources to motivate us. We need to know how to inspire ourselves and stay optimistic. This paradigm cannot be achieved in one day. Like any other muscle in our body, our mind is also a muscle, and we need to learn how to use this muscle effectively to attract only positive thoughts. Self-motivation can do a lot of good to us. We will eventually learn how to handle our tasks without panicking. We will soon become independent and will not rely on there for guidance. There is a myriad of videos available on the net which can provide us assistance.

XXXVI
Win Over Procrastination.

Introduction

Suppose you are working on a Friday afternoon and you are going against time to complete the work before the deadline in the evening. But while doing the work, you suddenly think that why didn't you start the work sooner? The answer to this thinking is Procrastination. And suddenly, you lose your focus.

Procrastination is a trap, and it is one of those traps in which many people fall. According to research, 95% of people around the world procrastinate up to some level. Therefore you are not alone. However, once you start procrastinating and start focusing on the things which cannot affect the final result, there are chances that the final result might not be in your favour because of your focus on trivial things.

Are Procrastination and laziness similar?

Procrastination is often confused with laziness. However, these two concepts are very different. Procrastination is a process where you select to do something other than the essential task. Whereas laziness is related to staying inactive and unwilling to do a task.

Procrastination generally involves ignoring a task that is important instead of doing a task that provides you with more joy and happiness. Procrastination is a serious issue because if a person procrastinates for a long duration of time, then they can become demotivated and disillusioned with their work. Moreover, if you procrastinate more, there are chances of depression and even job loss.

Procedure to overcome Procrastination

Recognizing that you are procrastinating

Sometimes people get confused with the idea of Procrastination. Many people think that giving up one important task for doing the other important task falls under Procrastination. However, this is not Procrastination. But if you start putting things away indefinitely or change focus because you wish to avoid doing something, then probably you are procrastinating.

Another reasons which might show you are procrastinating are:-

Scheduling your day with things that are not important

Leave an item on your to-do list for a long period of time.

Reading emails several times without making a decision.

Begin doing a high-priority task and go on coffee breaks.

Occupy your time with an unimportant task that other people have asked you to do.

Waiting for being in the right mood and right time.

Think about why you are procrastinating

One of the things you should do is think about why you are procrastinating before tackling it. For instance, if you drop a job because it is boring and unpleasant, you must focus on getting away with the job quickly. You must focus on the aspects of the job you find enjoyable.

The other reason behind Procrastination can be the lack of organization. The people who are organized in doing their tasks can successfully overcome Procrastination because they have prioritized their work by creating to-do lists and schedules.

However, even if you are organized, you can still be overwhelmed by a task and become doubtful about your abilities to do a certain task. Thus to overcome that, you need to put it off by doing work that gives you comfort.

The focus of adopting anti-procrastination strategies

One of the things that a person should do is forgive themselves for Procrastination in the past. Studies have displayed that self-forgiveness can help a person feel more positive and stop Procrastination in the future.

The second thing a person should do is commit themselves to do the task and not avoid it. To begin with, you can write down the task you need to complete and specify a time for doing them.

Once you complete a particular task, promise yourself that you will treat yourself with something like a piece of cake or a coffee from your favorite coffee shop.

Peer pressure certainly works. If you have concentration doing a certain task, you can ask one of your friends to watch you. Because with the help of peer pressure, people can achieve certain things which they don't think they will be able to achieve anytime soon.

Reduce distraction while doing the important task. When doing a task that challenges you, you should have a hundred percent focus on doing it. Thus to get the complete focus on the task, you need to stay away from distractions.

Tackling Procrastination if you are disorganized.

If you feel you are procrastinating because you are unorganized, then the following tips mentioned below will certainly help you in reducing your Procrastination.

Start organizing your work by creating a to-do list. In this list, you should write work according to priority.

Prioritize your work using Eisenhower's urgent/important principle.

Focus on becoming a master of scheduling and project planning.

When your focus is the highest, then at that time, you must focus on tackling the toughest task.

Create time bund goals for yourself.

XXXVII

5 Healthy Habits May Help You Live More Than 10 Years

Modern day medicine has increased the life expectancy of humans by almost 20 years that it was before. Now, this is mainly because of the ability to cure diseases and treat patients more effectively. But in the olden days, some people used to live to make it more than 100 years. This was possible in a time when modern machines for scanning and modern day medicines were not available at all. This was possible only because of the lifestyle that the people followed at the time. Now, it is possible for you to live longer as well, not by taking more pills or anything, this is possible by natural means as well. This article will outline five healthy habits that may help you live more than ten years longer than usual.

Eat healthily.

Eating healthy is more of a rule than a healthy habit. If you are going to eat high-fat junk food regularly, you can kiss away the dreams to live longer. We are what we eat. If we eat foods that are bad for us, then obviously our body is going to have adverse effects. Eating healthy is the bible for people who want to live longer. Think of it in this way. Our ancestors did not have full cheeseburgers or pizzas at the time, and yet many of them were more healthy and fit than most of the people that we see today. Food is not something that just satisfies our hunger; it is something that provides our body the things that it needs to function efficiently like minerals and vitamins and so on.

Meditate regularly.

Keeping a healthy body is one thing. But keeping a healthy mind is another. Both of these are linked. If you are fit and you are not mentally strong, and at peace, you will not live long. Things like stress and anxiety have adverse effects on our bodies. They cause insomnia, loss of appetite and a lot more things that will slowly reduce the years that you will live. Meditation helps you keep track of how your mind is performing. It helps you find some peace in the very high-speed world of today. Many monks that have lived for more than a hundred years all attribute the feat to the years of meditation that they do.

Exercise more often.

You can only be alive as long as your body can bear to keep you alive. Though this might sound like a harsh statement, It Is the reality. If you do not treat your body right, your organs will be in no shape to support your dreams of a longer life. The best way to ensure that your body is up to the mark is to keep it fit. We might have all heard about Darwin's theory. In short, it essentially means that any body parts that have not been used for a long time will wither away and that is the truth. So, keep your body younger and healthier by exercising regularly. This is most important if you are engaged in a job that requires that you sit for a long time daily.

Do not pop pills unnecessarily.

Another bad habit is popping pills. It does not matter if they are just vitamin supplements or natural herbal pills. Pills are pills no matter what and popping them without a prescription is plain wrong. People have become accustomed to an easy and pain-free life that many are not willing to face the slightest bit of pain or inconvenience for even a short while. Over the counter drugs for pain relief have a bad effect on people that they do not understand. If you at all want to live longer, then you have to stop taking pills without the prescription of a registered medical practitioner.

Quit smoking and alcohol.

Smoking and drinking are considered social evils in many countries and are also banned in many others. Alcohol is like a poison for your body, meaning that your organs have to work overtime to make the bad effects of alcohol go away. Smoking is not healthy. Your lungs were made to breathe in air, not smoke. Many people are addicted to recreational drugs as well as alcohol and these practices reduce the life expectancy of a person by many years. So, if you want to live a longer and healthier life, then take proactive measures to quit smoking and drinking today. Though it will be difficult, it will ultimately feel great.

So, these are some tips that people should follow if they want to live for a bot longer on this earth. So, follow these, and you will be there for your loved ones for a long time.

XXXVIII

10 Exercises to Gain a Muscular Body and Look Attractive

Exercising is an essential aspect of keeping your body trim and fit. Just being on a diet will not save you healthy, you need to exercise your muscles so that they can become stronger and not just wither away. Many of you might not be going to a gym or may not want to go to a gym for many reasons. This article will feature some of the exercises that will help you gain a better and muscular body and help you look more attractive, and most of them can be done at your own home. SO, check out the complete article to see what these exercises are.

Skipping.

You might think that skipping is something that only kids do for fun, but that is not the case, skipping is a trendy cardio workout that many adults do as well, it will help you lose some weight and also tone your leg muscles. They can also be a fun thing to do with your kids and will help them stay fit as well. Do some skipping and see how much you sweat.

Push-ups.

This is one of the most basic exercises that anyone can do. All you need is, well a floor under you. Push-ups are a very good exercise that exercise your core, your shoulders as well as your arms. Doing some push-ups frequently will help you develop a better-toned body. If you are finding it difficult to do a full push up, then you can do some half push-ups for a few days.

Pull-ups.

Again, pull-ups are a significant exercise that are focused on your shoulders and your hand muscles, including your biceps and triceps. All you need is a bar that can support your weight. If you think they are a daunting exercise, then go easy for the first few days and take some form of support.

Leg raises.

Everyone might think that leg raises are very simple, but try doing 3 or 4 sets of 25 reps each, and you will know why they are not. Leg raise can help tone your thigh muscles as well as your leg muscles.

Calf raises.

The calves are a major muscle group that is a problem for many people, the problem Is that calf raises are kind of painful, but they are essential if you want a muscular body. All you will need is small , and you can do calf raises.

Plank.

Planks are quite painful, especially for people who have just started working out. If you can do more than a minute of planks, then I say you are good to do even more. Planks help to focus on the muscles in your core and are important if you are looking at getting some abs.

Cycling.

Cycling is a great cardio exercise; it does not matter if it is outside or a fixed cycle in your house. Cycling helps tone the muscles of your legs and also help you to lose unnecessary weight and fat. Plus, cycling can be fun, especially if you can do it outside in the morning, you will not only end up feeling refreshed, but you might also be able to enjoy some of the scenery near and in your city.

Half crunches.

Half crunches are a great exercise if you want a flat stomach fast. This is because all of the pressure when you are doing crunches goes to the ab muscles in your body and also some on the core. The more crunches that you can do the better.

Bicep curl.

If you want a muscular body, then you will definitely have to work on your biceps. Bicep curls are the most definitive exercise for your biceps. Though you will have some pain after a few hours, the pain will be worth it when you look at yourself in the mirror. If you have some weights (dumbbells) at home, you can do some good bicep curls and reap the benefits of the exercise.

Running.

Running is an exercise that everyone should be doing. It does not have to be a 20-kilometer run on the first day; you can gradually go from a few kilometers to a lot. The benefits of running are many; it helps you increase your stamina, it helps you tone the muscles of your legs and thighs, it also helps you to lose some fat.

These are some of the exercises that people can do from the comfort of their homes without having to spend money on a gym membership, if you want to go more advanced, like becoming a bodybuilder or something like that, then it is advisable to join a gym and speak to a good trainer.

XXXIX

10 Foods to Lose Weight Quickly

Weight is something that everyone on this planet is very deeply concerned about. Not all of us have high metabolism rates that allow us to eat whatever we want and not gain any weight whatsoever. But there are foods that can help you lose some weight fast, especially if there is a wedding around the corner and you need to fit into that beautiful dress. So, read on to find out more about these secret foods that will help you lose that extra weight quickly.

Leafy green vegetables.

Well, this is one of the best ways to lose weight and quickly. Leafy greens like spinach, lettuce, collards and so on are a boon to people who want to lose weight quickly. They not only contain a lot of essential vitamins and minerals, but they also make you feel full though you have eaten less. This in itself will make you eat lesser calories because leafy greens by themselves have very fewer calories.

Boiled potatoes.

Many people would not find this as an ideal option on a list that is for weight loss foods. But boiled potatoes can do wonders for your body. They have a lot of nutrients, and they can make you feel full with a smaller number of calories. They are one of the most filling foods on the planet. Many gym-goers and bodybuilders eat boiled potatoes to maintain their weights in limits that they should be having for competitions and such.

Soups.

Most meals with low energy densities are good for weight loss because they tend to make people eat fewer calories. Soups are one of the items that fit the bill. Soup is essentially water, so you are filling yourself with water, which has no calories. Almost anything can be made into a soup, just add a little more water and a little more spice and flavours.

Celery.

Many people hate celery because it tastes very bad when eaten raw. But if you want to lose weight very quick celery is for you. Celery actually contains negative calories, as proved by some research studies, which means, that by eating celery, you are actually burning more calories. This is because your body has to do more work to digest celery than it normally does to digest other foods. But it might not be a good idea to eat only celery all day because you might miss out on other required and essential nutrients.

Cottage Cheese.

Also known as paneer in many countries, cottage cheese is a food that is high in dairy forms of protein, meaning it makes you feel fuller than you actually are. Protein in any form will make you feel full, and dairy protein is a natural form that is not only good but is also easily available and will not burn a hole in your pocket.

Avocados.

Many people think that avocados are to be avoided if you want to lose weight, the fact of the matter is that avocados are a very good food to help you lose weight because they are loaded with healthy fats. They have a lot of fibre as well making them less energy dense than people usually think. If you are making guacamole, then it might be better to avoid the chips and have a more calorie friendly alternative.

Cinnamon.

Though this is technically not a food, it is a spice that can increase the rate of your body's metabolism. This means that by just consuming this spice, your body is burning more calories than usual. Plus, cinnamon is something that you can add to almost anything: your coffee, your morning bowl of cereal and so on.

Coconut oil.

You are having a spoon of pure coconut oil before a meal can do wonders for your weight loss program. This is because coconut oil makes you feel full and content faster. This means that you are not going to eat a lot of food. Coconut oil has also been shown to help in reducing belly fat in humans.

Fruits.

Fruits are an amazing food to help lose weight. They are tasty, easy to eat and can be carried almost anywhere. Instead of snacking on some fried snacks, if you are consuming some fruit, it will help you lose weight. This is because fruit mostly contains water. And well, that fills you up.

Nuts.

Though nuts are high in fat, they do not actually make you fat. The main fact is that when you are eating nuts, you are not eating other fried snacks like burgers or French fries and that alone is enough to lose some calories. Eating nuts in proper quantities will go a long way in helping you achieve your weight goals, fast.

XL

10 ways to lower your blood pressure naturally.

Blood pressure is an important parameter that determines how healthy a certain individual is. Blood pressure related problems are slowly rising in the world today because of a variety of reasons like lifestyle changes, food conditions, exercise routines and so on. Blood pressure is usually manageable by taking daily pills. Though this option is available, it is never a good idea to take pills for things that can be controlled naturally. Blood pressure is one such thing that can be controlled effectively with a few steps. This article discusses ten ways that you can lower your blood pressure naturally.

Exercise.

Exercise is the number one cure to almost all problems that humans face today. A fit body is a healthy body. And this fit body is achieved by regular exercise. Something as simple as taking a morning walk for 20 or 30 minutes will help you lower your blood pressure in a natural way.

You are reducing the sodium that you consume.

Salt is a commodity that is present in every home and kitchen. One of the biggest causes of people having high blood pressure is the amount of salt that they consume. This is because different people process sodium in different ways, meaning too much salt might be a problem for you and not for others, but it is still a good idea to cut down on salt or use some low sodium alternatives.

Cut down on your drinking.

One of the major causes of high blood pressure and many more problems in the body is a result of excessive drinking. Drinking alcohol has been proven to raise blood pressure in many people, and it is a good idea to avoid alcohol if you are a high blood pressure patient.

Manage your stress in better ways.

Stress is something that naturally raises someone's blood pressure. Unnecessary stress is a huge factor in determining how effectively you are managing your blood pressure. Try to relax more so that your heart is not that worried.

Try meditation.

Meditation is a boon for humans, especially ones who are having high blood pressure. Meditation helps you control your mind and your body in a more efficient way thereby giving you more control over how your body reacts to stress or any difficult situations. Meditation does not mean you sit in a room for hours; it can be as simple as doing a few breathing exercises for 10 or 20 minutes a day.

I am eating more foods rich in potassium.

Potassium and sodium have many interactions within the body. One of them is: Potassium is helpful to get rid of excess sodium from your body. This means that it reduces the sodium levels in your blood vessels. Some of the most common foods which are rich in Potassium are bananas, apricots, avocados and so on.

Lose weight.

High blood pressure will obviously put more stress on your heart. And if you are obese, then this only worsens the already bad condition. Try to lose some weight by going on a good diet or going to a gym. This will not only make you more active, but it will also help keep your blood pressure in check. If your blood pressure is too high, then you might have to consult a doctor to tell you about friendlier exercises.

Eat more dark chocolate.

Well, though this might not seem to be a good idea, it actually is. Dark chocolate and cocoa contain an ingredient that is called flavonoids. These are helpful in dilating your blood vessels so that the blood pressure reduces. You should not eat a ton of chocolate, that will only worsen the condition. But little amounts will definitely help

Berries.

Yes, the good tasting berries are actually good for your heart. Next time you feel hungry and want to snack on fried food, consider having some berries instead. Berries contain polyphenols. These are good for your heart and also help you maintain good blood pressure. Not only this, studies have shown that eating berries often also decrease chances of contracting any other heart-related disease.

Eat foods that are rich in Calcium.

Most people who are diagnosed with high blood pressure often have low levels of calcium in their body. Studies have shown this interaction in many people. Calcium is pretty easy to consume; having a glass of milk once or twice a day will go a long way in gradually reducing the excess blood pressure in your body.

So, these are some of the best ways that can be followed to reduce your blood pressure back to normal levels. Moreover, these methods are all natural, and you will not have to spend a fortune on medicine that you will probably have to take daily.

XLI
Self Help Tips to Fight Diabetes:

Diabetes is a chronic medical condition, and it is a situation where the blood glucose levels of your body are very high. Glucose comes from the food that we eat, specifically sugar, and Insulin is another hormone that creates glucose into energy to give into the cells. There is also a condition called pre-diabetes, where the blood sugar concentration is high but not as high yet to call it diabetes. Diabetes is a serious condition and can cause very serious damage and problems to the body and the organs. There are specifically two types of diabetes, Type 1 Diabetes and Type 2 Diabetes.

General tips to fight diabetes (Irrespective of Type):

Heart diseases and strokes are one of the main reasons that tell us that diabetes can be very serious and fatal. How to control and lessen the risk of the fatalities:

Quit tobacco if you consume or smoke it.

Always make sure that your blood pressure is at the standard level of 129/79.

Healthy lifestyle options and choices need to be made for effective protection.

Consult your doctor in case of emergencies and ask his suggestions as to whether or not you need a daily aspirin or not.

Some tips related to other major reasons and their prevention are:

Stress related to life or other areas of work needs to be controlled and needs to be sorted.

Cope with the stress and find out the reasons for the stress and think about how you can reduce it or how to distract yourself from it.

Exercising helps as it helps to reduce stress, keeps you distracted from other tensions, and also it helps to keep and maintain a healthy lifestyle that you very much need.

Dieting does not always help, so instead of choosing to diet, you should choose better food choices so that they help to not only make you healthy but also helps to eliminate and control your bodily functions and fight diabetes.

If you can't decide on a meal plan, then speaking to a professional dietician can be of great help.

A lot of times, your blood sugar measuring equipment will be able to detect the increase and decrease and will help you keep informed about the status at all times. You must remember it check it at definitive times of the day like when you first wake up or before/after meals or even before and after exercising or whenever you feel queasy about it.

Regular appointments with doctors is also a really good way to keep diabetes in check. Remember to ask relevant questions to the doctor and ask him about the progress and the possible time within which to take the medicines if any and also inform him about the eating habits and other specifications.

You also should always keep your moods in check, for example, getting depressed, or sad or blue also helps to increase the risk of diabetes affecting more. Other symptoms like trouble in concentrating and overeating or insomnia also affect the risks of getting diabetes and making it a more serious problem than it already is. You need to make sure that when such things and symptoms do happen to pop up, you need to stay positive about it and handle it with care.

Suggestions and help from a professional doctor with a hand of expertise in this area might be the best thing to do. You can sit with the doctors and chalk out a well maintained and balanced diabetes plan which will include the daily routine, like the drugs and the medicines that are required for consumption, the daily goals and targets that need to be set and achieved and also the people you should and you need to associate yourself with in times of need.

Another very common thing you can do is join a support group. This is a concept that is followed in the western parts rather than here, but support groups for various diseases and conditions, even other than diabetes, helps a lot. The positivity and the openness in a support group is exactly as is required by the people and talking and sharing experiences and problems with them will not benefit to uplift your mood but it will also help you to learn from other experiences, and it will also help you to listen to advice given by others to you for the future.

Another thing is you should never get worked up or tensed after the diagnosis of diabetes in your body; you need to calm down and remember that it isn't just a disease, it's your life. You need to think of ways to overcome it and not think of negative things and give up. By thinking positive more than half of your problems will get over.

XLII
A Super Meal Plan For Diabetes

Following a meal plan for diabetes can ensure that you are getting their daily nutritional needs. It can also help you lose weight and prevent surges in blood sugar level. A diabetes meal plan is all you need to keep track of carbohydrates and calories intake and make healthy eating choices. Although no one plan will suit everyone, before creating your customized meal plan, you must know how food affects your blood glucose level.

Food and Blood Glucose- The Correlation

Food has a direct effect on blood glucose, and some foods raise blood glucose level more than others. An important part of making a diabetes meal plan is knowing what and how much to eat while helping to control blood glucose. The 3 main nutrients found in foods are carbohydrates, proteins, and fats, and you must regulate their intake to manage your diabetes.

1. Carbohydrates

Carbohydrates are the family of starches, sugar, and fiber in grains, milk products, and sweets. They raise blood glucose faster than other nutrients. Knowing the number of carbohydrates in a meal is helpful for blood glucose control. Choose carbohydrates from healthy sources like vegetables, fruits, and whole grains (high fiber).

2. Proteins

Proteins are a necessary part of a balanced diet and can prevent you from feeling hungry. They do not directly raise your glucose like carbohydrates but can make you gain weight. In people with Type 2 diabetes, protein makes insulin work faster, so too much protein is inadvisable for them. Use 15 grams of fast-acting carbohydrates that contain glucose is the preferred option.

3. Fats

Fats are a necessary part of a balanced diet, but although they do not raise blood glucose, they are high in calories and can cause weight gain. Make sure to include a small portion of fats in your diet, especially healthy fats from fatty fish, nuts, and seeds.

Guidelines for Healthy Eating

Eat a wide variety of foods rich in nutrients in each meal. It must include healthy fats, lean meats or proteins, whole grains, and low-fat dairy in proper portions.

Choose fiber-rich foods such as fruits, vegetables and whole grains like bran cereals, whole wheat pasta, and brown rice.

Try food alternatives to meat such as lentils, beans, or tofu.

Choose calorie-free beverages such as unsweetened tea, coffee, or water.

Choose substitutes for sugar.

Choose low salt food options.

A Generalised 24 Hour Diet Plan

1. Early morning

Start your day with a glass of lukewarm water to flush out and remove the toxins with a small teaspoon of methi seed powder.

2. Breakfast

Unsweetened tea or coffee, preferably black

A bowl of oats porridge (with milk or spices) and a whole cucumber.

A bowl of muesli with milk and a salad of cucumber or tomato

Wheat flakes with milk and a salad of cucumber or tomato

A bowl of vegetable daliya or upma

2 chapatis with 1 bowl of sabzi made of any green leafy vegetable such as spinach, radish, methi and a cup of curd

2 slices of whole wheat bread and egg white omelet with lots of boiled and sautéed vegetables.

3. Mid Morning

Instead of keeping a long gap between your breakfast and lunch meals, have a mid-morning snack:

A cup of green tea with a small handful of roasted grams or channa.

One whole fruit like apple, pear, orange,2-3 slices of papaya or guava (Anyone)

4. Lunch

1 bowl of salad and 2 rotis with 1 big bowl of vegetables and 1 bowl of dal, sprouts, curd or buttermilk,and 2-3 pieces of chicken or fish for a complete meal.

1 big bowl of vegetable daliya or khichdi with curd or buttermilk.

OR 1 bowl of salad made with 2 cucumbers, 2 tomatoes, half a bowl of brown rice and 1 big bowl of vegetables with 1 bowl of dal, sprouts, curd, buttermilk and 2-3 pieces of chicken or fish.

5. Evening snack

1 whole fruit like apple or pear or orange or 2-3 slices of papaya or guava.

1 handful of chana (boiled or roasted)

1 glass buttermilk (without salt or sugar)

1 sandwich (avoid using butter, cheese, and mayonnaise)

6. Dinner:

1 bowl of salad made with 2 cucumbers and 2 tomatoes.

2 rotis with 1 big bowl of vegetables and 1 bowl of dal, sprouts, curd or buttermilk with 2-3 pieces of chicken or fish.

1 big bowl of vegetable daliya or khichdi with 1 bowl of curd

7. Bedtime: You can have 2 walnuts or 4 almonds with a glass of lukewarm water before going to bed to reduce late night hunger pangs.

XLIII

Most Effective Food Habits to Gain Weight in a Month.

Many people in the world are underweight. Being underweight does not necessarily mean that they are people with malnutrition or something like that. Being underweight could also mean that they are not eating right. A lot of people might be underweight because of various reasons. Now, in this article we will focus on some of the reasons why people are underweight and what can the underweight people do to help gain more weight.

Eating healthy

Now, eating more is the primary weight gain method. But the most important thing that people forget about eating food to gain weight is that they have to eat the right food to gain good weight. Well, eating a ton of junk food like burgers, pizzas and French fries might make you fat soon, but they are dangerous because they make you fat. The weight that you are gaining from these foods is primarily bad fat. This might lead to problems like cholesterol and diabetes later in life. So, eating junk food is not the right way to go. But what is the right way? It is eating healthy food.

When you are eating healthy food, you are not building the amount of fat in your body. Instead, you are increasing the mass of your body, the useful ones like the muscle mass. This is actual weight gain that is supposed to happen. When you gain healthy weight, you will not face any problems later on in life. That is why you should eat healthily. Eat food which is dense with calories. Food like brown rice, whole grain foods and also nuts are all examples of good food for healthy weight gain.

Work out.

Well, it may be strange to see that working out is on the list of good habits to gain weight. The truth is that bulking up is a very good way of gaining weight. Many bodybuilders eat thousands of calories each day so that they can maintain their muscle masses. Now, you can gain weight effectively when you are doing some form or the other of strength training. Strength training is when you are lifting weights and such so that your muscles get bigger and denser.

Meaning that your muscle mass will be increased when you are doing such activities. It does not have to be weight lifting exactly, it can also be things like yoga or aerobics. All these increase your muscle mass.

The main thing why working out is on this list is because working out encourages you to eat more food. If you are underweight because you do not have a good appetite, then the workouts that you are doing will help generate that appetite for you. It is obvious that when we work out, we feel hungrier, this means that, if you are hungrier you will be in a position to eat more. So, make a proper diet plan with foods pre and post workout. These foods should contain ample amounts of protein so that your body's muscles can rebuild themselves and can grow.

You are eating at the right time.

Eating is one thing, but eating at the right time is another important thing. Things like protein which are the building blocks of our body are important at the right times. The reason for this is that proteins or amino acids cannot be stored by the body. This effectively means that when the body needs protein, it absorbs it from the food that we eat and does things like repairing our muscles and building new muscles and so on. Now, because it is not stored for future use (like how carbohydrates or fats are stored), the body will ignore any excess protein.

Meaning that you should provide the body with protein at the time that it needs it. Well, we cannot exactly know when the body needs protein, but we can approximate these timelines based on our daily routine. People who go to the gym usually drink a protein shake once they are done; this is so that the body can absorb protein. All the lifting that they do is what causes muscles to tear (microscopic ones).

These need to be fixed by the body, and that is when it gets the protein from the protein shake. Now, when you eat at the right time, your body is also ready to digest the food based on the time. Meaning that it does not starve until you are eating the next time. When you eat food at the right time, the body can increase your appetite at the same time for the next coming days.

It is always a good idea to visit a doctor if you think you need more guidance on weight gain. Some people have genetic problems which only doctors can diagnose and recommend a diet for.

XLIV

Nutrition Requirements for Optimum Performance

As an athlete, your first priority is your performance. Nutrition plays a huge role in ensuring that you are delivering the optimum performance during your stints. The key to delivering an optimum performance is an active lifestyle, physical fitness, and meeting the nutrition requirements. If you commit to eating healthy then you will get the energy that will help you enjoy sports or even run to the finish line without going out of breath. In case you are not getting enough proteins, calories, fluids, carbohydrates, vitamins, or even irons then you will be delivering a poor performance and even get tired easily.

In this blog, we will be talking about nutrition requirements that professional athletes need on a daily basis. As much as intake of proteins on a daily basis is crucial, carbohydrate and water intake also plays a crucial role in keeping the body healthy and working. While sweating it out, make sure to keep your intake regularly to avoid draining out.

Nutrition requirements and diet for athletic professionals

Even though the diet of an athletic professional isn't much different from that of a healthy person, the different food portions depend on three key factors. The kind of sports he or she is involved in, the intensity of training the professional undergoes, and last but not the least, the total number of hours you perform on a daily basis. The key is to not consume more calories than you can actually burn so it is always advised to not consume more energy than you can spend on your performance every day.

Always remember to never burn calories on an empty stomach even though everybody's body is built differently. Given the uniqueness of everybody's body built, there are two things which you need to remember before you work out. The amount of food which is the right amount of food for you and when the right is time for you to eat before you start exercising.

Carbohydrates and their need

To gain energy and exercise on a daily basis, consumption of carbohydrates in the right amount is very essential. Usually, carbohydrates are stored in the liver and the muscles. Pasta, rice, whole-grain bread, and even bagels are foods rich in complex carbohydrates. They are low in fat and provide vitamins, fiber, and even minerals along with energy to the body. Simple sugars including soft drinks, jam jellies, and candies contain a lot of calories but aren't very nutritious in nature. The key is to ensure that a little more than half of your calories every day should come from carbohydrates and consume them before you exercise.

Proteins

For healthy muscle growth and to ensure that the damaged body tissues are getting repaired on time, proteins are a must. But that also doesn't mean that a protein-rich diet will help you promote muscle growth. Only relevant strength training and regular exercise will allow your muscles to change and grow. Proteins are an accessory to muscle building alongside strength training. Always remember that eating too much protein will get stored as fat in your body. It also increases dehydration in the body and leads to calcium loss. In addition to that consumption of proteins in excess can also put unwanted pressure on your kidneys.

Water and fluids

For athletes, water is one of the most essential nutrients and most of the time it is overlooked. Fluids including water not only keep the body hydrated but also maintain the right body temperature. Every day through vigorous exercise, there is a lot of water which your body loses out in the form of sweat. In case you are looking for ways to keep your body hydrated then you should start by drinking plenty of fluids including water with meals. This rule needs to be followed with or without physical exercise. The key is to drink 2 cups of water prior to physical exercise. This will ensure that your body is not getting dehydrated while you are sweating it out in the gym. In addition to that, while you are working out, it is advised to continue sipping water from time to time. If you decide to switch to an energy drink after the first hour of physical exercise, then your body will receive the necessary electrolytes.

The trick here is to consume fluids including water even when you don't feel thirsty.

Conclusion

While you are practicing for your performance, eating nutritious food in the right quantity plays a key role in ensuring that you deliver optimum performance. It is always advised to go with a professional dietician in case you are looking forward to enhancing your professional performance. Consumption of nutritious food will ensure that your body is reacting well to the extensive exercise and training that it is going through on a regular basis.

XLV
Physical Exercises For Optimum Fitness Levels

If you are not a big fan of weight lifting or serious physical exercising, but you also want to sweat it out so that you fit it into your clothes back, we have got it covered for it. We all know at times sweating it out can be intimidating especially if you are alone. So how can you lose weight without weight lifting? Which exercises will help you to fit into your old clothes right back? How long do you need to invest in each of these exercises? We have got answers to all your questions relevant to physical exercises which will help you increase your physical fitness and reach its optimum level.

The key to keeping your body fit and lean is sweating it out regularly at least 4 to 5 times a week. But having said that, every time you decide to run a couple of miles on the treadmill or even pick up some of those weights, you will have the urge to head straight back to your sofa. Now here's the catch, what if we say some exercises don't require you to run miles like you are preparing for a marathon and you still get to lose weight and stay fit. Some workouts ensure your body remains healthy and you can reach optimum fitness levels with consistent efforts.

In addition to keeping your weight in check, it will also enhance your body balance, strengthen and protect your joints and bones and even wave off some of the bladder issues.

Swimming

It is probably one of the best physical exercises which are liked by a majority of people across the world. It is known to take the stress off your joints as the buoyancy of the water supports your body throughout the swim. In addition to that, it also allows you to move your body in the water with ease. It is less painful especially for people who have arthritis and similar joint problems. There have been several types of research conducted on swimming and its effect on mental health. The majority of these research studies have shown that swimming can improve mental health and put people in a better mood.

Along with swimming, you can also give water aerobics some serious thought if you suffer from incurable joint problems. Both these physical exercises help you to burn some easy calories and tone up your body with time.

Strength training

Strength training has got nothing to do with bulky muscles and lifting big weights. Lifting lighter weights allow your muscles to become toned and strong. The key is to keep our muscles working so that we do not lose their strength with time. Muscles also help people burn calories and the more muscles we have, the more calories we burn thus our weight is maintained over time. Studies have shown that strength training helps brain function to remain preserved over the years.

The key to effortlessly performing strength training is knowing the right forms and techniques. The trick is to start with lighter weights and move onto heavier weights by a pound or two after a week or two.

Tai chi

Tai chi is a Chinese martial art form that allows both the body and the mind to relax. In addition to that, it also includes movement of the body thus keeping it in shape and fit. The martial arts form has several graceful movements and the change from one form to another is very smooth and graceful. There are several levels of Tai chi, thus making it a martial art form that is accessible to people of all ages regardless of their fitness levels. Since balance is an element that is enhanced during the classes of Tai chi, it is particularly recommended to older people who with age lose their balance and stability.

Kegel exercises

Even though they do not directly help you to sweat down your extra pounds, they strengthen your pelvic floor muscles. For those of you who do not know what the pelvic floor muscles do, they support the bladder. Kegels is popular among women, although men are also considering it as an important physical exercise with time. The key to performing the exercise correctly is to squeeze the muscles like you would when you are preventing the urge to pee or pass gas. Hold the position for two or three seconds and relax your muscles.

Walking

Even though walking might feel very simple, it is quite powerful. It reduces cholesterol levels, strengthens bones, and also keeps blood pressure in check. In addition to that, it also helps you to live your mood and reduce the chances of diabetes and heart ailments. The trick is to invest in a pair of shoes that support your feet when you set out to walk in the morning or evening.

XLVI
Sleep Habits For Optimum Health

A good night's sleep can help you conquer the world every day but to do so, you need to make certain changes in your current lifestyle and behavior. If you are having trouble sleeping at night, then your days are also not energetic enough to get you through the end of it every day. Sleep foundation laid down statistics about insufficient sleep stating that around 35.2 % of adults don't get an adequate amount of sleep at night. In addition to that, due to insufficient sleep, they feel sleepy throughout the day and lack the energy to perform well.

Half of the American citizens feel sleepy during the third day of the week to the end of the week due to insufficient sleep. This is one of the main reasons why adults are recommended 8 hours of sleep at night to avoid waking up exhausted or spending the entire day sleeping. It has also been noted that chronic poor sleepers have an upper hand and a higher risk of developing cancer and dying from it too. The key is to have enough sleep during the night so that you wake up feeling well-rested and have enough energy to go through the day without feeling lethargic and sleepy.

Here are 8 sleeping habits that you need to incorporate into your daily lifestyle and behaviors to get a good sleep at night.

Sleeping habits for a good night's sleep and optimal health

Since having a good sleep at night is relevant to sleep hygiene, you should assess that properly to find out the flaws in your sleeping style and schedule. All you need is a healthy and nutritious lifestyle and certain behavior changes to help yourself sleep peacefully at night.

Setting up a consistent sleep schedule

The key is to go to bed at the same time every single day and wake up in the morning at the same time every single day. If you are consistent with your sleep schedule then your body clock will also get adjusted to the same thus helping you to fall asleep when it's time. This is one of the main reasons why nurses and flight attendants have trouble getting a good sleep at night. Due to their work commitments and the lack of having a proper daily schedule, they end up having an unstable sleep schedule which prohibits them from having a good sleep at night.

Creating a regular bed time routine

If you are a bath person before you go to bed at night, then make sure you do that every single day. If you have to listen to music before sleeping then make sure to plug in your earphones every day at night before sleeping. The tip here is to remain consistent with your bedtime routine so that your body doesn't identify any sudden changes and becomes alert instead of resting and slowly falling asleep.

Getting regular physical exercise

It is always advised to shed some sweat through physical exercise every day regardless of whether it is hitting the gym, brisk walking, performing any sports, or just strolling around the garden.

Maintaining a healthy diet

One of the main reasons why it is difficult for people to fall asleep at night is their meals. It is very important to note what you are having as your last meal of the day because it could aid or prevent your body from properly digesting the food. Although you could have a snack before you head to the bed for sleeping.

Avoiding nicotine and keeping a check on caffeine

Both substances are known to affect your sleep schedule negatively. Once the nicotine users break the cycle and have experienced the withdrawal symptoms, it has been noted that they can easily fall asleep compared to those who use it regularly.

Avoiding alcohol

Since alcohol happens to be a sedative that slows the activities of the brain. Even though it allows you to feel sleepy, it will prevent you from having a good sleep at night as you might wake up frequently and even experience nightmares throughout the night.

Keeping your nap timings short

Usually, throughout the day your body builds up sleep debt, which helps you to fall asleep peacefully at night. Naps are thus clearing off the sleep debt in minutes and hours but they can also interfere with your proper sleep schedule at night. Thus, it is always advised to have naps of 30 minutes and not more than that during the day.

Using the bedroom for sleeping only

The key is to not use electronics, eat or even watch television or OTT shows in your bedroom. If you want to have a good sleep at night sleep then you need to ensure that your bedroom is cool, quiet, and dark.

XLVII
Yoga and Pranayama

Pranayama happens to be a yogic practice that focuses on the breath of an individual. If we are to consider the meaning of the word pranayama, then "Prana" means vital life force while yana means to gain control. In addition to that in the yoga culture, it also means to enhance life energies. The pranayama is mentioned in Hindu religious textbooks including Bhagavad Gita and even Yoga Sutras of Patanjali. Although later, in Hatha Yoga texts there has been a completely different meaning of Pranayama as suspension of breathing.

Prana happens to be an essential element without which our bodies will not be able to function. It keeps our mind and body healthy and alive. There are several types of Pranayama mentioned in several ancient Indian Hindu texts and stories. It consists of breathing techniques that can be practiced by all without requiring any specific skillsets. In this blog, we will be talking about everything related to pranayama and the different kinds of breathing techniques that will help your mind and body to function better.

Benefits of Pranayama

There are several benefits of Pranayama and if performed right regularly it could enhance life by increasing the quality of life for people. The benefits include increased energy levels along with increasing and enhancing the quality of prana. In addition to that, it also clears chakras and nadis, therefore, enhancing the aura and spirits of people performing the different breathing techniques. If you are performing pranayama regularly then you will become calmer, enthusiastic, energetic, and more positive.

A positive and calm state of mind will enable you to take better and smart decisions and will make you less impulsive and more thoughtful. In addition to that, it introduces harmony between your body and mind. It increases the spiritual, mental, and physical powers of people. Last but not the least, it enhances the mind by providing more clarity and brings good health to the body.

Types of pranayama and how to perform them

Kapal Bhati Pranayam or skull shining breathing technique

This breathing technique is considered to be one of the most important types in the lot as it is used in detoxifying the body and even clearing the energy channels. It also helps the body to create and experience more positive energy.

Bhramari Pranayama or bee breathing technique

If you have a lot of things going on in your mind, then it is time for you to try the Bhramari Pranayama a try. It will help you to quieten your mind and is extremely beneficial for those who suffer from hypertension and anxiety. All you have to do is find a quiet room to prevent your brain from overworking.

Nadi Shodhan Pranayama or Alternate Nostril Breathing Technique

If you are unable to focus on work or have lately become attentive then you need to perform Nadi Shodhan Pranayama for nine rounds. You can follow it by meditation for some time to relax and focus on your priorities better. It calms the body and mind along with allowing both the hemispheres of the brain to perform better.

Bhastrika Pranayama or bellow breathing technique

If you are low on energy then by practicing bellow breathing technique you will be able to reach higher energy levels. You will become a high performer with more energy.

Things to remember why performing pranayama yoga

Make sure to monitor your breathing accurately while you are performing the different breathing techniques. It is always advised to practice pranayama and other yoga postures under proper guidance. Make sure to have a yoga tutor in front of you while you perform the different breathing techniques for guidance. Do not make your body extremely rigid or jerky while you are inhaling or exhaling air. Always identify and understand your capacity to perform over exhaustion and injuries.

If you perform yoga and pranayama, then it is always recommended to perform yoga asanas first followed by different types of pranayama yoga. Always perform shavasana before you perform pranayama to relax and calm your breathing. Do not perform any exhausting yoga postures after performing pranayama. All you have to remember while performing pranayama is that it is performed to gain more control of your breathing. If performed right it will detoxify your body.

What is the best time to perform pranayama?

Usually, pranayama and similar breathing exercises should be best performed on an empty stomach or a couple of hours after you have consumed food. In addition to that, you need to perform the different breathing exercises after at least 30 minutes of drinking water. It is always advised to perform pranayama before sunset and only tranquilizing pranayama can be performed before going to bed at night. You can drink water after some time and continue with your regular schedule without any preventions.

XLVIII

5 Reasons Why Continuing Education and Training is Beneficial

Introduction

Continuing education is a concept of pursuing post-secondary education or doing programs that adults pursue after formal education. The continuing education can vary from seminars, one-time classes, and online courses to entire degree courses. Few professionals require continuing education in different ways.

Some of these requirements are from yearly classes or tests which keep you in line with the current trends in the industry.

Other professionals need continuing education in the form of degrees which prepare them for new opportunities and responsibilities. Moreover, some people even attend seminars, conferences and lectures to help employees learn from other experts in their field.

Continuing education is a highly appreciated concept. Personalities such as Warren Buffet and Oprah have supported continuing education to better human skills. Moreover, Barack Obama, the former president of the United States of America, has often quoted that reading for an hour a day at the White House helped him immensely grow his knowledge.

In this article, we will mention the six benefits of continuing education for you as a professional worker in any industry.

Enhances your chances of promotion

Employers around the world want to hire and promote a person who is demanding to grow themselves. Hence, a person who plans to continue education will portray to the customer that he is willing to become at what he does. This might prove to be beneficial for him because there are many employers who take continuing education a positive step and thus promote such people.

Moreover, since a big company has plenty of positions, there are many vacancies that can only be taken by advanced degree holders. Thus with an advanced degree, you will have a greater number of options to apply for getting a job.

Also, having an experience of continuing education will put you above your competition; thus, continuing education enhances your chances of impressing the hiring manager. Moreover, continuing education also helps you in handling more tasks in a better way.

Increment in salaries

Since you will become more knowledgeable with continuing education, the chances of earning higher salaries at a new position also increase. According to research, on average, a college degree holder will be able to earn twice more than a person who doesn't have a degree. Even though continuing education requires you to invest money, your return on the investment will be of high worth.

For getting more pay, pursuing a bachelor's, master's, or doctoral degree is highly beneficial for employee benefits. Also, according to the Bureau of labor statistics, advanced education of any kind increases your chances of getting higher incomes. Thus continuing education is highly beneficial for professionals from a different classes.

Gives you an opportunity for career transition

If you are planning to get into a new field, it is often observed that continuing education assists you in getting into the field of your choice. From nurses to accountants, every profession requires some kind of degree to get a respectable job. Thus obtaining these degrees will make you prepared for moving into a new career.

Moreover, in certain streams, continuing education is extremely vital because these streams require you to learn specific skills crucial for becoming successful. Thus, there's no alternative for you to become successful without this training.

Continuing education improves your image and marketability.

Continuing education is an essential component of your resume. Moreover, in many jobs continuing education is an immediate qualification requirement. However, even if your job doesn't require you to have continuing education, having additional knowledge about a field is always beneficial.

Suppose you apply for a job. Now, if you have a continuing education degree, then there are more chances that the employer is able to recognize you because you have a degree that others don't have. Moreover, with a continuing education degree, an employer thinks you have more knowledge of current trends and skills needed in the industry. Also, with continuing education, you would have learned some new skills as well.

Enhances personal development

Even if you are completely satisfied with your life, it doesn't mean that continuing education isn't for you. As experts have said that learning is a lifelong process; thus, giving time to continuing education can be a journey of personal development.

With continuing education, you will be able to learn more about a subject which you find interesting or for which you require some additional skills.

Thus there are skills which you can use from continuing education for your own advantage. Moreover, even if you plan to pursue a course for fulfilling your hobby, continuing education courses can give you the advantage of advanced learning on the track of becoming a better person.

XLIX

7 Relationship Management Skills That Will Enhance your Business

Introduction

Whether you manage a company with several employees or a start up with a small customer base. Constructive relationship management skills will always put you out of the league with the competitors and help you build a customer base.

In this article, we will explain a few relationship management skills that will help you in increasing the customer retention rate. These relationship skills are for every professional working in the managerial fields of different companies, irrespective of their experience. So let's begin.

Staying vigilant about the customer needs

A key for a growing business is to be in line with the needs of the customers. If you are unaware of what the customers require, then you'll struggle to attract the attention of the customer and do business with you. Also, having knowledge about the industry's priorities is an essential component of demonstrating your values to prospects and nation-building.

One of the brilliant ways to learn more about the target market is through surveying existing customers about what they do and what they don't value. For doing a market survey, you can use different platforms such as Facebook. These surveys will help you in collecting valuable information.

Direct Marketing Skills

There are several businesses that carefully audit the money spent on customer acquisition, but not on time. Time is extremely valuable, and if you have the capability to quantify the value of time, then calculating relationship management ROI becomes easy.

For making your job easy, start learning the basics of direct marketing, starting from the cost of your time to improving the sales conversion rate. If you become a master of these concepts, then you will find yourself at a place where forming business relationships with new customers will become simple. Moreover, being a master in direct marketing skills will also help you in maintaining the already existing customer relations.

The capability of connecting with strangers

Reaching out to prospects and converting them into customers is one of the toughest tasks to master. Even the most capable and experienced salesperson finds it difficult in certain specific scenarios where the prospects have less interest in doing the business with you. Thus the capability to talk with strangers becomes essential.

Relationship management is highly dependent on the way you talk with strangers. A relationship manager should be comfortable conversing with people over cold calls to prospects they meet at trade shows and events. Moreover, the relationship managers should be an expert in conversion and persuasion to make relationship management easy.

Ambition and Motivation

For business people, being ambitious and motivated is highly essential. The professionals who are enthusiastic about reaching out to new prospects and getting in touch with existing customers to know what they are interested in helps them beat the competition around them.

Being ambitious in sales and customer service is not wrong at all. Instead, in the age where everything is becoming automated through chatbots, people desire to talk to customer representatives as they still believe talking to a human will be more beneficial for them when it comes to solving an issue. Therefore, with a motivated, ambitious and result-driven attitude, you won't find yourself struggling to connect with customers.

Knowledge of Sales funnel

In the business world, it is a lot more difficult to get your first customer than getting your second customer. Many firms struggle with relationship management because they are not able to acquire new customers at an appropriate price and pace for constant growth.

Thus one of the essential skills is acquiring new customers while still retaining the existing ones. The easiest way to do this is by an automated, systematic sales funnel.

Proficient Strategic Thinking Skills

When you are managing fewer customers, not having a strategy will also work for the betterment of the business. But if you are managing relations with a high number of customers, then an unsystematic approach will not work. You must have the prowess to form strategies for becoming successful.

Moreover, even when you are highly competent in customer service skills, it will be impossible for you to manage relationships without a solid strategy in operation. Because strategies can help you solve problems from simple principles to relationship strategies.

Knowledge of CRM software

When there is a problem, theirs is always a solution. The problem of managing thousands of people is huge. But the solution to the problem is the customer relationship software. With the help of customer relationship software, you can keep a track of the interactions you have with your customers across the entire organization.

A person capable of using CRM applications will provide a big advantage in maintaining relationships throughout different large companies and organizations. Moreover, a CRM expert will also give you the opportunity to form new relationships.

L

Seven Things You Must Remember Before Setting a Goal

Everyone wants to achieve something in their life, either for money or happiness or whatever they intend to the success of achieving. So the first thing everyone does to achieve anything is making goals. Everyone sets up a goal to achieve anything be it small or large, but the first thing everyone does is making a goal. You must be very familiar with the 'Let's go to the gym goal' which is mostly set on the 1st day of every new year and then dropped after a few weeks. There are other goals as well which are important to you and achieving it will have a great impact on your life.

But why do we need goals?. We know what we want to achieve we can start working and get to it. It is true, but in reality, it's not applicable. Taking the gym example again, we want to become healthy that's why we go to the gym. Here becoming healthy is what we want to achieve and going to the gym regularly is the goal. Without a goal, we don't have a direction towards our goal, and we will have a hard time achieving it. Goals are also required to check the progress towards your dreams.

Now that we have a dream and we know that we need to set a goal to make our dreams come true. But you need to keep certain things in mind before setting your goal.

1. The WHAT?

You need to set a goal for something that you want to achieve, so it is fair to think about what do you want to achieve. It can be anything like becoming a great writer, a musician, a scientist or whatever you want in your life. So take the first step and think about what you want to achieve or become in your life and then move forward with setting your goal.

2. The WHY?

Once you have answered what do you want to achieve you should also ask yourself Why do you want to set a goal?. It's fairly obvious because you want to achieve something that's why you want to set a goal. But the more important question is why do you want to achieve that particular thing. This need to be answered because it will serve as your motivation to complete your goal. Without motivation, you can only set a goal but can't achieve it because the human mind always needs a reason to do something with enthusiasm. So before setting a goal to ask yourself why do you want to achieve a specific thing.

3. The HOW?

Now you have done the thinking process about what to achieve and why to achieve but now let's move on to How to achieve your dream?. This is also a straight forward question, and its answer is also really simple- just set a goal and complete it. But it's not too simple you have to lay out a plan for everything, and you need to commit to it. You need to be productive and effective with the plan, and slowly you can achieve it. The plan should be concrete because a rough help won't be helpful for long.

4. Know what you already have

Let's suppose you want to become a theoretical physicist, but you don't have any idea about physics and anything remotely related to it. So you have to start from scratch, you need to learn about the motion, its laws and the forces in nature. So your goal should be according to your previous knowledge. If you already have a fair share of knowledge in physics, then you can skip the leaning the basics part and set goals accordingly. So note down what you already know and then set a goal.

5. Commitment

If you want to achieve something big you need to give your heart and soul into it. Achieving anything requires a commitment. If you are willing to commit to it then only you should pursue it otherwise there is no point in making goals and planning for it. At any point, you will have two choices, either to do some work which will help in the progression of your goal or not to do it and relax. This decision will decide the outcome if you always choose the first one the chance of succeeding will be much higher. While always selecting the second one will help you with nothing.

6. Take help from others

There is always a person who has already gone down a path which you are on, and he/she is aware of all the technicalities of the path and can help you with the path. They can make you aware of all the obstacles that come along the path and will also help you overcome them. So don't hesitate to ask for help.

You can also find a mentor. It will speed up your progress by ten times. But you still need to commit to it and give your heart and soul.

7. Set up a checking system

Let's suppose you are working hard towards your goal but how will you know about your progress. Hence you need a checking system to check your progress. This needs to be done before setting up a goal because after you set your goal you might want to start working towards it and at that time thinking about your checking system will disturb your flow. So you need to design it beforehand. You can check your progress weekly or monthly or whichever suits you best. A good checking system will be weekly because it is a short period and it will give you a good summary of your work. You can check your progress on Sunday and then think on it whether you are going in the right direction or not. The main advantage of weekly checking system is that you can improvise your work the next week if it is not up to mark.

Just make sure you have already dealt with these seven things before setting up your goal. After this, you can set up your long term and short term goals and get right into work to achieve your dream

LI
10 Tips to Build Trust Among Your Consumers

Your customers need to trust you to be able to purchase something from you. They need to believe that all your messages and quotes are accurate. Your selling should match to what you said it is and if anything does not work correctly then you will give support. But trust cannot be build suddenly. It is a time taking process to get your consumers able to trust you. Build relationship with customer so that they feel trusted with your company.

Here are some tips to build trust:

Improve Security: Your fist move is to make your consumers feel safe when they purchase from you. If you are selling your products with the help of ecommerce platform or even if you are not selling online but people may visit your website. The security in your site plays a major role to build trust and consumers feel free to purchase from you. They do not have to rethink or do a research before buying from you once they feel safe and trust you.

Be visible: You should be socially active to be visible. Being socially active helps in many ways like increase in visibility of your company or your products. More people get attracted towards your products and those people recognise your brand value. The more you expose your brand through social media marketing, the more people you get yourself to trust. Also social media is flexible. You can add new product's images, information or discount offers for your customers. The customers get to know more about you and it builds trust for your brand. The key to build trust is to be active on social media and reply people instantly if they have any query about your product. A good customer service always helps in building trust.

Less Promise and More Deliver: Customers tend to hate the brands if they feel they have been lied to or fake promised about some product. Any time if a customer feels they have been manipulated, they lost trust and they may never come there to shop or purchase anything. To fulfil your customer's expectations you should promise less and deliver more. This way you will never customers expectations. For example, if a product will take 3 days to ship you tell them it will take 5 days or if a product has validity of 1 year you tell them 8 months. This is the way your customers gain trust on you and you will never be in a position to break your promises.

Good customer service: When customers face any issue with a product or any service, trust becomes frail. If they face any issue and you give good customer services then they will always recognise your company and trust you. But if you fail to do so, you can lose a customer. Make your customers happy and they should feel like purchasing only from you the next time. Also try to give affordable customer services to your consumers.

Make your brand personal: To gain trust, make your brand personal. The employees should speak from their heart not by heard a script while interacting with customers. If your customers feel connected with your brand, their trust for you will become strong. Make a customer friendly environment and build relationship with customers.

Communicate: Do not make your customers feel confused or give them half information. Communicate more with your customers. The more you interact, the better. Be transparent about your missions or goals. If your customers find you holding details, it will imprint a negative effect. If something gets wrong, acknowledge your mistakes and give good customer support. This is the key to your customers trust for you. Also ask your customers if they are happy about the services. Be in touch with your old customers by giving them information about new products and offers.

Be available: It is very important for your brand to be available for the customers. If you include phone number in your website or make a page for instant chat, this can increase your conversation with customers and people will feel comfortable to talk with your representative with any doubts they have. Also you must have multiple contact options for customers. So they can contact you as per their convenience. For example some people prefer talking over phone and some people prefer talking over texts. So help both type of customers by having chat pages and telephone contact lines both. Your representative should be available at anytime. Make yourself reachable to your customers.

Do not speak industry lingo: Some clients may like your attempt to explain about the products or services in depth. But when you use more technical terms and your client do not have idea about the terms it results in confusion for clients. They end up not purchasing from you even though you are giving the best services. So speak less about technicality and make the conversation more friendly and understandable to the customers.

Respect the advisers of your clients: Always make sure your customers get the best advices when they seek help regarding any of your products. You build trust when you respect other advisers to whom your customers look for advices. When you describe the willingness to be a team player, your customer's trust towards you increases.

Offer things with no profit motivation: If you try to tempt your customers for your own profit, most of the time customers recognise the motive and they do not come back for any purchase. Offer services or discounts so that your client does not feel like being manipulated. They feel trusted and they come to only you for any purchase. Never try to fool your customers, try to be honest. Also do not make a deal for your loss. Always prefer deals which benefit both the parties. There is no priority than customer trust for a brand or company

.

"Strive not to be a success, but rather to be of

"Strive not to be a success, but rather to be of value." – Albert Einstein

LII
Effective Ways of Time Management for Success

Have you ever found yourself working day in and day out and did not get the results you expected from the efforts that you put in? Have you found yourself pulling an all-nighter just before your final exams? Or do you have a habit of procrastinating, more so during deadlines? Well, we are human beings after all. We sometimes do not understand the importance or value of time. That being said, according to a study, an average Indian's lifespan is 63 years. And those of that 63 years, only 8-10 years of your life are the time you get to spend freely, to actually do something meaningful; the rest just runs its course in doing regular chores like eating and sleeping and the rest is used to attend school and college.

So, isn't the time enough that we looked at life and realized the serious implications of our actions, our habits over it? To even begin with, we do spend a lot of time working, but most of the times, we are not really sure whether we actually utilized the time we had and were able to do our work effectively and efficiently. So, without further ado, let's jump straight into fixing this; let's learn how to use the limited time we have more effectively; the word for it is 'successful time management '.

Let's begin on this positive note by promising to oneself to effectively maximize our efficiency. All the successful people the millionaires and billionaires out there, they know how important time is and they have learned how to utilize it and become successful. So, let's start right away!

Start your day right: As the saying goes, 'Well begun is half done', beginning your day in the right manner tends to have an enormous impact on how that particular day goes on and how. It sets the pace of the day and gives you the required momentum to finish the day on a high note. There are various ways to do that: meditate, or even just prepare yourself for the upcoming day. Although, avoid opening your Instagram or Facebook right in the morning.

Have a plan for what you want to achieve: Plan out the way you want the day to go by. Make a to-do list. Think of all the important tasks to be completed and note them down somewhere. Although one thing should be kept in mind.

The number of tasks and the amount of work to be done should be realistic and that being said, you should always try to complete all these tasks on time. Also, do set time limits for each task.

Break task into reasonable units: We all know how tiresome a day can get just by thinking about the enormity of the looming tasks. Like the saying goes 'united we stand, divided we fall' so also will the tasks if you consider tackling them all at once. A better way to handle them would be to break these tasks into sub-tasks. When huge amounts of loads are broken into these small units, life seems much more bearable. Also, the sense of accomplishment will constantly provide you with the confidence and courage needed to go through the regular working day.

Prioritize your tasks: This is another aspect which most of us fail to keep in mind while doing work. After noting down all the task for the day, one should know which the most important job of the day and which tasks is should be completed before the day ends, without fail. Also, it's advisable to start the day with the most difficult task as one's mind and body are ready to start afresh and hence, efficiency is very high.

Avoid multi-tasking: Yes, you heard that right. Multi-tasking as efficient as it does sound, in reality, it is not. Since we are human beings and not computers. To emphasize this point let's look at the brain of the computer. It's integrated circuits or ICs are built with multiple cores to help them multi-task. But our brain is not built in a similar manner. Busting the myth about multi-tasking, it is in fact quite ineffective and even inefficient in tackling our day to day's work. It can even harm the brain due to the enormous amount of information it has to handle and work with.

Do not forget to delegate/outsource: You might want to impress your boss or head by accepting multiple responsibilities and not allotting or sharing it with your work-mates, but to be quite frank, taking help from colleagues and delegating them part of the work can help you manage your workload more efficiently.

Time for eating, exercising and socializing: Even though you might be a guy who loves to work and work, take some time off to meet your friends, or go to a restaurant, or order food online. Exercising early in the morning is quite effective in keeping you healthy and fit, both physically and mentally. This is because exercising and relaxing and socializing are things which help you feel stress free and hence be all charged up when you return to work.

Pomodoro technique: This technique was developed by a person named Francesco Cirillo sometime in the 1980s. It is a method which helps a person do his/her work more efficiently. In this technique, the user is supposed to set timers of a particular time- interval usually 25 minutes as practiced by the founder, although there is no restriction on that matter. During each of these 25 minute – periods called 'pomodoro', one was supposed to leave aside all the other distractions and maximize one's working efficiency and complete one's tasks. After every 'pomodoro' a small break could be taken to relax for a while. And after every few cycles or pomodoros, a slightly lengthier break could be taken to feel refreshed.

Be organized: Keeping things organized will help you know where to look for a particular thing in its time of need. You would not be wasting precious time and energy in its search.

Time for learning: They say that a person never stops learning until he/she dies, and they are right. Even successful personalities like Bill Gates and Elon Musk reserve some time every week to learn something new. And if they can, so can we. And it's particularly inspiring to follow in their footsteps.

LIII

Factors Which Affects Our Productivity Both in Negative and Positive Ways

This world has a simple rule if a person is productive then he moves towards his/her goals. Everyone has certain goals in life; some people want to become a writer, some want to be a software developer, some want to start their own business and many other goals which are dreamt by millions. But the important question in hand is, what are you doing about your goal? Are you working on it and moving ahead step by step by doing everything right and with effectiveness or you are stuck at a place and looking for some help in order to move forward or you are just sitting in comfort in your home and thinking about your goal and the success that follow after you achieve it whilst scrolling the never-ending list of shows on Netflix.

In the first scenario, you are doing your work according to the requirement of your goal and moving forward to achieve success, here you are productive ultimately. You have a plan of action, and you are following it. While in the second scenario, you have done some work, but you are stuck that means you have progressed a bit, but after some point you are stuck. In this case, you might have thought about being productive, but you haven't laid a solid plan of action.

You just have a rough idea which only worked for a shorter period of time. It will be redundant to discuss the third case because Netflix can help in so many ways of not being productive. Here you have a goal in mind, and you are imagining what will happen after achieving your goal, but no thought is given about the process of achieving your goal. For example, if you want to become a singer, then you need to start singing or if you want to become a writer then write.

First and foremost, you need to have a plan and a willingness to work before thinking about productivity.

There are many factors which affect productivity in both, positive and negative ways. So if you want to be productive and start working towards your goal, then you need to look into each of the factors which affect productivity.

You need to remove the negative factors in your life and build on the positive factors.

1. Distractions

The technology has evolved so much, but it also made a path for lots of distractions like Netflix, social media, YouTube, etc. Distractions are just like hurdles in the race towards your goal. You can either jump and dodge them, or you can remove them out of the picture. Removing distraction is much easier than learning to get control over them. Because these things are designed in a way that you will get addicted to them and it will be much harder to control it, so it is better to remove them out of your picture. But you obviously can't throw your stuff away. The best thing you can do is to remove them out of your sight like when you are working you can keep your phone or whatever feels like a distraction to you in another room. You can also switch off your electronic devices or mute them.

Removing distraction is one of the most important factors in productivity. So if you want to do anything, you need to get rid of all the things that can distract you or get you out of your flow.

2. Music

Classical music enhances your productivity. It is said to have a very positive effect on your productivity and effectiveness. Music affects the mood of a person that has a positive impact on productivity. You can also listen to other music as well, but it can also become a distraction. For positive effects, listening to classical music or a song on repeat is advised. Listening to random songs can cause distraction because sometimes we don't like a certain song so we then go on to change song which can disrupt our flow.

3. Environment

If you work in a clean and distraction-free environment, then you can focus on your work quite easily. You must have experienced it. When you study in a library, then you can actually understand things easily but when you study or work in your room which is untidy and full of distraction you have a harder time completing or understanding anything. The environment has a direct impact on our mindset. So keep your environment clean and distraction free.

4. Planning

If you plan things well beforehand, you will have a much easier time working towards your goal. But you need to make a well-detailed plan of action to boost your productivity. A rough plan can only help you for a short period of time. To make a plan, you need to understand what are the important things which need to be done in order to make progress towards your goal. There are some things which are urgent, but they don't affect the progress so much. So you need to identify the important things that should be done and give them more priority than the things which are urgent but don't have a big impact on your progress towards your goal.

5. Exercise

Exercise has a lot of impact on individual life, both physically and mentally. It helps in uplifting the mood and creates a positive mindset which helps us in focusing on our work and thus increasing productivity. It also increases the functioning of our brain cells which helps in understanding and doing difficult things quite easily. Not exercising has a negative impact because you become lazy day by day which leads your mind to delay your work.

6. Food

Eating good food affects our mood greatly. It can pull us out of any bad mood. So before working try on having some good and healthy food, it will surely increase your productivity. Eating junk food can help you with the mood, but in the long run, it has certain negative effects.

The rule is simple if you have a goal in mind or you want to achieve something you need to start working on it but just working without any direction takes you nowhere. You need a good plan and productivity. So, remove the negative and build on positive.

LIV
How Reading Habit Affect your Success and How to Build It.

Introduction

Since the time we start understanding humanity, education, human behavior, and other aspects, people constantly give us advice that reading books will undoubtedly enhance your mind set and motivate you to achieve something productive in life. Moreover, many people believe that books can be a great source for learning new things because life is all about learning from other people's experiences irrespective of whether they are positive or negative.

Also, it is believed that many people assume the hardest working person to be in a library studying a book which interests them the most. To be successful, you should be able to implement the learnings of the books in your practical life. However, simply being a keen reader won't be sufficient for ensuring your success. In this article, we will explain the various ways how successful people benefit from reading.

People who read books have increased focus.

A common trait you will observe in people is their focus on doing a certain task with complete dedication and motivation. Reading is considered a quick process; however, it is not singular. Readers naturally take breaks during reading.

However, a sincere reader won't put a book down for longer than a day if they find it extremely interesting. This trait of not putting the book down even for a single day is similar to the successful people who don't give up on tasks which come to their table.

Setting up goals.

With focus, readers set goals for themselves whenever they sit and start reading the book. The goals can be based on different things such as setting the number of pages they will read today, the number of chapters they wish to complete in one sitting or focusing on solidifying concepts until it is understood. Thus a reader who sits for reading a book always sets a goal before reading. Thus, a person learns the importance of setting goals through reading books. Thus setting goals is an essential aspect for successful people in achieving what they desire, and reading books can be the best way to help them master the strategy of setting goals.

Spending time efficiently

Suppose there are 15 minutes before a person wants to go somewhere. Hence, instead of doing something unproductive, the person decides to read an article which is a trait of a successful person. Successful person always values their time and focus on investing in doing something productive because doing something productive will help them learn new skills or achieve a goal. Because they believe with every minute they waste, the opportunity of learning goes waste.

Successful people have a perspective.

A person who reads a lot has a plethora of knowledge about different issues. That's why you will see that a successful person is always able to handle difficult situations with ease because they have a plethora of knowledge about the various aspects of life. Because when you read, as a reader, you start thinking about a situation from the reader's point of view. After putting yourself in the reader's place, you start figuring out the various alternatives in which you can react to a particular situation. Thus a successful person is proactive in handling situations which is extremely necessary for problem-solving.

A reader has a reflective attitude.

Along with gaining perspective on different issues, the readers also reflect on what they read. Meanwhile, having a perspective allows a person to observe the situation from the other side. Staying reflective allows them the opportunity to understand how they can become productive with their new perspective. A person who is successful doesn't see reading as just reading words. They know the value of words written in the text and what effect it will have on their mindset.

Readers have incredible reading and writing skills.

The greatest orators in the human history have been extremely enthusiastic about reading. It can be clearly observed that people who have considerably cemented themselves in the human history have been keen readers such as Nelson Mandela, Lincoln, etc. Moreover, successful people also draw inspiration from their role models and utilize the inspiration to further their cause.

Readers have increased memory.

A good reader always knows the power of the brain. Theoretically, a brain can hold an infinite quantity of information. Thus the more you read and learn, the easier it becomes to retain information. Successful people don't believe in the fact that learning new things pushes the old out. They simply believe that continuing to learn expanses the knowledge, and with the prior knowledge of an older technique, they understand how the shortcoming of that technique is fulfilled by the newer technique.

"Life is 10% what happens to you and 90% how you react to it." – Charles R. Swindoll

LV
How to Choose an Idol to Be Successful

Everyone looks up to someone who is successful, who inspires them and who make them believe that success is possible. It is like a fuel to perform in the long run. We want to become like our idol and we want them to progress too. Having an idol also signifies a positive mind because instead of being jealous we are taking inspiration from a person who is successful and we want them to be more successful. An idol can be quite important in our lives because they inspire us and let us do whatever we want to be in our life. We try to relate their successes and failures with our success and failures and seek motivation in case of failure and joy after every success.

Most of us have celebrity role models like an actor, a scientist or an athlete etc. We see their achievement and it creates a surge of energy inside us to do hard work and achieve our goals and dreams. You can also have a role model that you know in real life like your teacher or your mentor. Mostly their achievements and talents inspire you to work harder for your dreams or you want to have a positive mindset like them or whatever you are looking for, the main thing is an idol act as a fuel for your inspiration so that you can constantly work hard to achieve your own dreams.

Choosing a known Idol

It is better to choose an idol that you know in real life rather than choosing a celebrity Idol because you can take advice from them easily because you know them in reality. You should choose an idol who will help you become successful and your best version. He will help you and guide through to your success. Having an idol will increase your speed towards the path of success.

But before choosing an idol you need to look into yourself first and you should look for an idol accordingly. Because just looking for an idol without any purpose is redundant and it won't be of any actual help towards your success. So look into yourself, identify all the negative traits and habits that you exhibit and write down every bad aspect of yourself. It will help you see what is the main problem with you and the things that you need to work on in order to improve yourself.

Write down all your long term and short term goals and your dreams and what person you want to become and what you want to achieve in your life, it will help you look for a suitable idol for yourself. You should also try to build some confidence in yourself because it will be helpful in getting good advice from your idol because your idol will only help you when you want to be helped which is shown by a bit of confidence. Having a positive mindset while taking advice from your idol will make it easier.

After looking into yourself and realizing what you want you should look for an idol who have achieved what you are willing to achieve. You can take their advice and follow their footsteps in order to become successful. But don't choose your idol only on the basis of achievement. You should look for someone who is a good human being too. A good idol will know himself or herself and they don't pretend to be someone else. A good idol should be just their natural self.

Another positive trait to look in a good idol is that they don't wear you down, they will praise you for who you are and they will try to uplift you in every possible way. So don't choose someone who makes you feel down. A good idol always remains in his/her best behavior with everyone. You can consider someone who is not at the top of his field because the top performers take risks more often so it will be safer to go for someone who has worked hard and remain consistent and then tasted success.

Choosing a celebrity as an idol

This is very common among young people. They idolize a celebrity and fill themselves with the urges to achieve something great. You can choose any celebrity who you like just make sure that they are good as a person too. Because people tend to attach emotions to their celebrity idol which can result in negative ways. So try not to attach emotionally and try to use a celebrity idol for positive things only like inspiration. The positive side of choosing a celebrity idol is that they always show their positive side to everyone and most of them have certain life principles which they follow. But the negative side is that we can't take direct advise from them but mostly they give enough helpful advice.

Choosing an idol is good whether it is a celebrity idol or an idol that you know. The only things that matter is that you should use this opportunity for positive things only. Learn about their success and failures and try to look at what measures they took when they failed in order to become successful. This will help you during the setbacks while pursuing your own dreams. You can also look for some personal faults in your idol and see how did they overcome the effects of these fault in their path of becoming successful.

Another thing to keep in mind that you should just take tips, advice, and lessons from your idol. Don't copy them completely because the things they have done might not work out for you but taking tips and lessons and keeping them in mind will surely help you in your path. Try developing your own style instead of transforming yourself into some other persons. Just take the advice and learn from their mistakes, don't follow them blindly. Just improvise, adapt and overcome and have faith in yourself.

LVI

How to Convince Anyone According to Your Decision

We all have moments in life where we are faced with the daunting task of convincing another person, be it your mother, your best friend, your teacher or a customer. I say 'daunting' because persuasion is a tool which can seldom be successful, although if one has a few tricks up his sleeve, anything is possible. For this to happen, the person must be one with amazing communication skills and an ability to connect with other people and make them see what you want them to do.

Persuasion involves a lot more psychology than you'd probably imagine. Persuading or convincing a person to understand your decisions is a formidable task at best. But since research has been done and the subject of persuasion has been understood, let's not wait any longer dwelling on the past and let's be prepared to be able to convince anybody anytime.

Some of the techniques and things to keep in mind while persuading anybody are:

Attitude amplification: Persuasion is all about how a person would look at the persuader and hence it becomes extremely necessary to have a few qualities like confidence in oneself and a firmer attitude. This is because the degree by which they will be convinced or swoon by you are largely dependent on the confidence in your tone and how much they were moved by you. Speaking with a soft attitude will help you reach nowhere. So next time you want to tell your boss.

Conversion: If you're opinion is supported only by a minority of the people, you have a higher chance to persuade a person with a different viewpoint. People who believe in what the majority believes in are mostly people who go with the flow. These are the kind of people who don't have a strong motive to believe either side of the argument, hence, they can be persuaded easier than the rest.

Information manipulation: A better exchange of knowledge can lead to higher chances of convincing a person successfully.

If the information is transferred to the other person quite clearly and understandably, and in completion, the person is more likely to trust you.

Sincerity and truthfulness will also play a major role in convincing the person. Being honest leads to the development of trust, and if the other person trusts you, then definitely convincing him/her is much simpler.

Relevance of the subject matter to the other person again is another parameter that would be important to note, as this leads to the person paying more attention and therefore more interested in what you are saying.

Also, the manner in which you tell someone something is kind of the most important factor here, as it is extremely necessary to understand the feelings of the person you are trying to convince. Just saying all you know blandly, without any emotional attachment will definitely not help you convince other people. Hence, the manner in which information is transferred should be noted and controlled.

Priming: If you're a person who understands people, you will know that a person becomes much more involved and interested if you involve the person in conversation and make him come up with answers to the information, rather than you just telling him. Priming is the method of telling a person something by not telling him everything and not so much as directly. If the information is given in such a way that the other person is forced to think and make a guess, the person better understands your idea and is easier to be convinced.

Obligations: If a person helps you in your time of need, wouldn't you be thankful to them and be obliged to do the same when they need help? Whenever you owe someone, you will be obliged to listen to them and will be convinced by what they say. So also, in your case of convincing others, it is much easier if the person is obliged to listen to you. In short, being a nice human being would definitely help you achieve those goals and these people who are obliged to you for something good that you did them, they will respect you and you can definitely convince them.

Scarcity principle: According to this principle, people are more likely to get convinced by you if you provide them with a piece of information that regards something which is not quite easily accessible or available or something that might get over soon or that there aren't enough of the things left.

Ultimate terms: While actions speak louder than words, words are sometimes a more powerful tool than any. It is the proper usage of 'certain' words in certain situations which can change the tide in your favor. Make sure to keep yourself knowledgeable about these things and strike when the iron is hot.

Respect: Finally, it boils down to the most important aspect in convincing a soul. Forget convincing, it is quite necessary to respect and be respected to even have a conversation let alone convince somebody. A few pointers below on how to tug the rope and just convince anybody:

Have a respectable conversation. Avoid arguments and definitely do not get down to exchanging blows.

Respect other opinions as much as you want them to respect your own. It's a give and take.

If you do commit a blunder, do not hesitate to accept your mistake and apologize emphatically.

Involve the other person in the conversation and give him/her more opportunity speak. This is to avoid the person from being left out of the conversation.

Sympathize with the listener and try to see the world through their eyes. Hence you will know how to convince the person.

Appeal to the nobler motives when all else seems to be failing.

Make the person believe it was his own idea. It becomes much easier from there on

The basic motives that help people get convinced are Profit, Pleasure, Power and Reputation. So, make sure to nail your points correctly and lastly remember: A person will buy only from a person he likes, trusts or respects. Best of luck in the long journey of convincing and persuasion!

LVII

How to Inspire People Around You

Everyone looks up to someone, either for inspiration, for courage, or just look up to a figure who shares the same beliefs as they do. Motivational speakers, leaders, and activists all share the same outcome; they want to inspire everyone around them. Inspiring someone for the right cause can lead them to perform better, care better and form strong opinions that they will stand for. It can also bring a positive change around us. You can also follow some steps to inspire those around you, whether it be your close friends or a large group of people.

Stand strong on your beliefs.

The first step to inspire others is to inspire yourself first. You should stand strong on what you believe strongly in, only then can you voice your concerns, your thoughts and ideas and make it more compelling to the masses. These issues should be close to your heart, and you have to show them you are not afraid to stand up for it.

Speak your mind.

Be persuasive on what you want to convey. Your speech should grip your audience with as much anticipation, like as if they are going to achieve something great. Make them believe that you and they can conquer battles together.

Be the best version yourself.

If you love something passionately and want to share your passion with others, you will find a way to voice your beliefs. But first you have to make sure that your behavior and mannerism and reputation is at par with what you believe in, otherwise, if there is a contradiction in what you are saying versus what your actions were, you will quickly lose your followers.

Challenge them.

It is safe to just sit back and listen, but if you challenge them to take action, then they will try their best to go to great lengths to prove and fight for what they want. Keep some expectations from them, and they can be sure to deliver.

Care about your followers.

Now that you have a good amount of followers, always care for their wants and needs also. Give a lending ear when they need anything, from advice to queries to doubts to everything in between. The only way you can keep them close is to care about what they are trying to say too.

Share stories.

It's one thing to tell, it's another thing to share. Giving your followers an insight on your past success and failures will bring them closer to you and your goal and make them believe that you're a human too, just like them. Share your stories of risks and challenges you had faced before, so they will also be well equipped with that knowledge if they too cross the same path in future.

Give them the strength to change the course.

Inspire them to have courage and faith in what they are doing. Convince them that if they take an effort today, they can collectively change the future for tomorrow. Work towards that common goal together to achieve greater things in life.

Speak the truth.

No matter how unpleasant reality may be, you will earn more respect if you speak the truth than hiding behind lies. They say the truth will set you free, hence this is precisely why false claims will not get you far.

Share the credit.

Getting from one point to the other is a shared victory. Even if you are the primary instigator and the leading force, without the joint efforts of your followers, you would not have made such an impact. Share credit where credit is due.

Be positive.

Even if things don't happen your way, always keep up a cheerful face. If you falter, then your followers are sure to lose their faith in you. There are always hurdles and obstacles, but you have to push through those and stay positive despite the odds.

Build up your character.

More than your reputation, focus more on building up your character. Your character is what you are and will be in their eyes. A strong and good character makes for a great role model.

Heal your followers.

No matter their past, if they have joined your cause, you should see past what they did and help them build a better future for themselves.

Make them feel good about themselves.

If they have achieved something substantial for your cause, acknowledge it and give praise. Make them believe that what they did will inspire others to walk the same path too, and together they can achieve greatness.

Stay calm.

Do not crack under pressure. Being weak will only result in failure to your cause. Take criticism and hate with stride and do not let the hate get you down. More importantly, do not be a quitter.

Share what has inspired you.

Sharing your influences can give your followers insight into what shaped your thoughts and ideas. Give credit to books, quotes or speeches that you have come across as a foundation for others to look into it as well.

Keep your promises.

Do not make promises you cannot keep. People will look up to you for something they too can get in return. If you do not keep your end of the bargain, you will lose all that built up trust and support.

Explore alternate ideas.

Challenge your beliefs every day. There are no correct answers to anything. Differences in opinions will form, so that is why it is important to keep an open mind and explore alternate thoughts and ideas.

Give equal importance to everyone.

Favoritism will not work here if you're a team and you have to work together. Even if someone is a few steps behind, treat them as part of your family. After all, they have stood by you no matter their output to your cause.

These are some of the ways you can inspire others around to make a positive change, not just for themselves but also for their society, and working together for a common cause.

"Personal development is the belief that you are worth the effort, time, and energy needed to develop yourself." – Denis Waitley

LVIII

How to Make an Accurate Decision in 10 Minutes.

Every day, every hour, every minute leads us to take decisions. It could be something small and trivial, or something crucial. Decision making could be for self or for someone else. But the factor remains the same; that any choice you make will lead to a certain outcome, whether good or bad or right or wrong.

Choices that are taken at home or at the workplace require more attention since we have to build up our surroundings. Our decisions have to let us move forward in life. These two areas are the key components in our lives.

Below are some tips and tricks to help you make quick and accurate decisions.

Do not overthink

Some of the time, we have more choices then we need. Excess of anything can crush us and lead to explore our options less. So in this case, try evaluating your choices simply as good or bad, which will make things easier and quicken the procedure of weeding out the less optimal decisions. This limited method is perfect for the over-analyzers who insist on questioning every variable.

Identify your risks

Recognize your regular habits that have become routine. These are some of the things that require very little thought on your part because they're automatic. Then, take some time to focus and reevaluate which choices might be harmful or unhealthy and create a proper plan to develop better daily habits. Familiarity breeds comfort. There's a good chance you were making some poor decisions simply because you've grown habituated to your ways and you don't think about the danger you're in or the hurt you're causing.

Focus on the present

More often than not, we are overcome by the big picture, trying to see how our choices will affect the future. This can take the best of us and makes us mentally drained because you're trying to see each step along with its every consequence. In order to overcome that, save that energy for the task at hand,

and try and make the best decision possible. Make a choice based on what might make the next step the easiest instead. Live in the moment and don't fret about the upcoming future.

Put a worth on your decision-making time.

Break each minute into ten slots. Based on how much money you make per minute, determine the monetary value of six minutes of your time. Don't spend a lot of money and time on decisions that will not have a big influence on your work or finances. To find out how much time and money to spend on a decision, you may also find it helpful to consider the following:

The impact our decision will make on other people.

The impact of it on your place of work.

The financial bearings of the choice.

Your level of accountability for the decision.

The consequences of poor judgment.

Find a strategic objective.

You may reduce the number of criteria that bear on your decision if it helps. Although you may have multiple measures to achieve with the decision, you should try to distill the key criteria into a planned objective. Your objective should justify one or two of the most important criteria.

Don't wait around for the perfect choice.

Instead of waiting around for an ideal choice, figure out which principles are the most crucial for you for making an adequate decision in your favor. If you find yourself waiting for a choice that meets your ideal set of values, you would most probably end up doing research or think deeply about the decision for a very long time.

Pick an option and go with it.

Since there is never enough time to contemplate the future consequences of every little decision, which might be unknown, you should just choose one option. As long as you have eliminated all the bad choices, you should just pick one of the results and run with it, because at the end of the day, taking the proper action is what should be done.

Get over your fear of decision making by looking at the consequences of inaction.

If you are afraid or think twice about the concerns of making the wrong decision, it is important to work through this fear. To get over your fear, you could instead reflect on the long term consequences of not making that particular decision. Once you have gained a new viewpoint on the serious consequences of inaction, you should just go ahead and make the decision.

Use the 10-10-10 method.

Take a step back and look into how you will feel in ten minutes, ten months and ten years. This way, you can get some new insight on how the most important decision could impact your short, near and long term future.

Acquaint yourself with alternate solutions.

If you feel that the two choices you have at hand do not meet your expectations or that both feel inadequate in terms of meeting your goals, you may want to generate a list of substitute solutions. Give yourself five minutes to think about a list of alternative solutions to your problem.

Figure out what you really want in the final outcome.

You may want to figure out what you want the most out of your decision at the end of the day. You may want ways of making more money, or maybe living in a particular place is more important to you, these choices could help you come to a decision.

Consult someone about your decision.

Have a chat with a close friend or colleague about the decision. Explain your goals and criteria clearly. Ask for their opinion on what you should do and listen carefully. By talking through with them on the decision and explaining your overall goals, you should be able to get some insights on the issue.

Hopefully, these tips and tricks will help you sort out your decision-making skills and you might be able to make quicker decisions in the future.

LIX

How to Be an Interesting Personality?

A person can have an interesting personality when he/she have the traits that aren't being possessed easily by anyone and are rare to find. By coming across various minds, I have found these following traits to be counted as interesting.

1. Risk Takers are always attracted to the viewer's eye:

It takes a courageous heart to become a risk taker. Risk takers have their goals very precise and clear with themselves and are never ready to compromise with the quality of the product that they are going to get in the end. They always pursue the path don't look for the alternative. I rarely can think of anyone who takes the safer or easier route. People who spend their free time watching TV or playing a video game or X-box or slouching on the couch the whole day I find them uninteresting; they are not likely to gain everlasting experiences. Being an element of interesting personality cannot be completed at all without the element of risk.

2. Curiosity:

The future always belongs to those who are curious to know and learn new things, and this curiosity is what makes them interesting. Curiosity is the key behind every new idea. And the world is starving for the innovators.

3. Opinionated:

A person who has his own opinion is always out of the crowd, which makes me him easily attractive and interesting. His opinions are listened to and valued if he can put his views forward in the right way. Forming an opinion is good but persuading your opinion to others is not good.

4. Presence of personality is mattered:

You are interesting at a node when you find that people realize your absence in the crowd.

5. Having a good sense of humor:

Good sense of humor is a cherry on the cake. It not only makes your company lovable but also makes you a good personality.

6. A Friendly attitude with the rest of the present members:

Being an arrogant person with an attitude of no use makes you an irritating person. Instead, if a person has a friendly attitude, he/she will be loved to listen and will be found as interesting too.

7. Development of New Skills:

People will find you interesting if you are helpful to them anyhow. Hence, by developing any skill which is also helpful for the rest, you can be interesting.

8. Be a Good Story Teller:

Make sure you are expressive and have a modulating tone so that people find it interesting to listen to you.

9. Ask Good Questions:

Asking questions and asking good questions have a difference in them. Make questions which make the person sitting in front you to think twice and ponder about your question relevance.

10. Follow what your mind says, and heart allows.

11. Read A lot:

A good reader is always a good speaker as he has the content to speak. He doesn't speak irrelevantly.

And those who have controlled the flow of tongue, are always waited to get listened because the listeners want to know What's there inside the box for them?

12. Spend time with more interesting people

The company you keep influences your personality. "If you are in the company of monotonous people, nerd people or serious people, you are more likely to become like them sooner or later. The same goes when you have the company of interesting people." It is the aura of people, the vibes which get emitted from them which affect us too.

Just consider a meetup with another group of people who are motivated to carry on their interests and passions.

13. Go thoroughly into one of your interests

You might be motivated to become a learner of many domains, developing a little knowledge about everything. Instead, consider knowing much about one topic and flaunting your fluency in that area.

April Fonti says she finds people interesting when they "really pursue one thing with great intensity and depth over a long period. They could be very successful scientists or just quiet loners. It doesn't matter."

14. Open up to people

That will be a rare person who does absolutely nothing and has a null opinion on any of the topic.

15. Creating Your style Statement:

It's nothing less than creating a brand; you will be easily distinguishable from the rest and definitely will be more interesting such that people like to get in touch with you. It doesn't mean always creating funky looks like Ranveer Singh, but it shows to be like Sonam, and Alia when it comes to creating a style statement and thus leaving your mark over the people's mind.

Being an interesting personality isn't a big task as long as you are ready to go out of your comfort zone and take some risk with a courageous soul.

LX

Morning Rituals for High Performer

Most people believe those morning rituals play a key role in determining how well will the entire day go by with time. Having said that, what experts mean to say is the chances of your life not being a snooze button from which you keep running from is high if you spend the entire morning snoozing your alarm. Most people avoid having a proper and nutritious breakfast in the morning because they are running late. Having said that since they are always running late and end up grabbing a piece of toasted bread on their way to work, the chances of them forgetting an important document at home is also high. What are the chances of you requiring that document in your 9 AM meeting? Possible and very common among corporate workers like yourself.

In case you are wondering how the top performers make use of most of their mornings optimally, then they follow some rules every morning without fail. We are mentioning these rules which you need to incorporate in your daily morning schedule to become a high performer if you haven't already.

Waking up from a good night's sleep

It is recommended by experts and doctors for adults to have a night's sleep of at least 7 hours to ensure their daytime performance is not hampered. Unfortunately, it has been noted that more than 30% of the adults living in America have trouble getting an adequate amount of sleep at night which prevents them from performing optimally during the day. In addition to that, not having proper sleep at night can also result in diabetes, obesity, stroke, several heart diseases, and even cognitive decline.

What we are trying to establish here is that without proper sleep at night, you cannot possibly become high-performance. Being consistent with your sleep timing and ensuring that your room is dark and quiet can help you get a good 8 hours of sleep at night.

Spending the morning quietly

Several types of research have shown that spending the morning quietly helps you get clarity in your life every day as to what your daily priorities, goals, and important tasks are for the day. Spending the morning in quietude helps you to figure out your day. In case you are wondering what to do to spend the morning quietly, then we have several recommendations for you. Right from taking a walk, working out, cooking yourself a healthy breakfast to writing down your daily to-do list, meditating, and even introspecting. What we do not recommend is using your phone as you are spending an hour of silence in the morning.

Smiling and positive thinking

Smiling in the morning releases positive neurotransmitters also called endorphins and dopamine which help you to have a good and happy morning. In addition to that, smiling also releases serotonin which lowers your heart rate, helps your body to relax, and prepares your immune system for the day. Also after you wake up, think of something you are grateful for. It could make your day better and you will feel like you woke on the right side of the bed.

Making your bed, every single morning

Leaving your bed unmade and messy not only makes your bedroom look bad but also prevents you from fulfilling your first task of the day. If you start your morning by making your bed, then you will find the motivation to perform different tasks throughout the day. Making your bed is a good start to winning the day and getting your priorities fulfilled and catered to for the day.

The key is to find your rhythm

Create yourself a morning routine of tasks, so that you do not have to spend time thinking about what to do next and procrastinate. The minute you start to procrastinate, you are going to avoid the actual task. You could wake up, drink water or any fluid of your choice, go for a job, come back and prepare yourself a breakfast, take a bath, get ready for work, and get started on the day. As much mundane as it may sound, following a daily morning routine could prevent you from procrastinating throughout the day.

Crafting affirmation every morning

A positive and powerful affirmation can go a long way. Why is this task important for you? What are your commitments? What activities help you to perform better in life? These are three simple questions, but knowing the answers to these questions is the key to becoming a high performer daily. Having said that, consider yourself more than just a regular working adult. You are more than that, more loved than you can imagine, and more powerful than you can think of. Right thinking and a good mindset can help you become a high performer every day.

LXI
Most Effective Ways of Academic Research

For academic research, the step wise step investigation and material study and sources to prove facts and conclusions all are vital. Students of colleges or universities must go for research in their domain subject to benefit themselves for the rest of the life. Research can benefit anyone whether from science background or commerce background. Every domain needs research to go in depth and explore more on the subject. Research is an important aspect for academic as well as professional careers.

A student goes through these questions before starting research on something:

What is the research for?

How to conduct the research?

What is the thing I'm going to observe throughout the research?

What are the preconceptions about the topic?

What is the expected time duration for the research?

Here are some tips to conduct your academic research most effectively:

Choose your topic: To start with your research, you must know your topic of interest. Choose something you are passionate about. The more you want to discover more about something, the more it leads to better research. Also you will be able to explain the research well to others. That way this topic will be worth for publication.

Organised: You already have a lot of work, assignments, extracurricular activities, your personal work etc do. This research work is something you are doing out of your interest. You have to schedule time for it. You have to be organised to make time for the work when you already have tied schedule with so many other works.

Time requirement: Make sure of yourself that you make time for your research work when you start your research. You should give a separate time each week for research work. Don't let other distractions take that time from you.

Make a to-do list: When you are into research work. Everything will go step by step. You have to plan your progress. Use white boards or sticky notes. Write down your to-do list. You should also plan a time duration for every work and be devoted to the time. You should make your progress in the research by following your plan to lead the research effectively.

Plan in segments: You can't finish the work if you think of doing it continuously. You need rest; you need time to think fresh. So divide your work in segments. Do each part of at different time. After completion of each segment, take rest. Also if you start fresh each time, you can easily find out the errors.

Research plan: Some people plan their research for 3 to 5 years. But if you are not into long research plan, make a plan of 1 year and divide your research plan according to that. However a good research needs time. Be patient. A work done in hurry will always result in incompleteness.

Strategy: whenever you have available time for research, do your research with strategies. Difficult tasks need more focus. So use your time effectively. Whenever you are available, sit with your research. Make strategies which are effective. The work with less intensity like editing or correcting or taking notes can be done in smaller time period. But the work with more difficulty needs to be allotted more time. Also free up your mind when doing any research.

Do something with your time: whenever you feel like you have some time, do progress with your work. No matter how small the amount is, but be spontaneous.

Start your work: when you are ready with your idea, start your works. Do not keep on postponing it. There is no right time for any work. The right time is now. Make a start to reach the destination. Write down the information or create a file in your desktop about the topic and go on doing it.

Organise in files: Never fill all the data in same file. Use different files for each work. It will avoid confusions.

Don't get bored: If at any time, you feel like bored. Stop the work and start later with fresh mind or do work in different parts and leave that part for later when you feel like doing it. The successful research needs your interest.

Deadlines are important: Work with a deadline for every part and try to meet those time limits.

Write in many forms: Once you are done with your research, write conference papers, journals, articles etc. This will make your knowledge go deeper.

Separate file for edits: Whenever you make corrections or edit something, do not mix up with old documents. Make separate file for edits. Do not delete any old data, you may need that later.

Publish: When you are done with the research, do publish it in different sites or journals.

Connect: As you publicise your research, make connection with other researchers. You will get to know more. Also attend more seminars, conferences to enhance your knowledge. We all know knowledge is never ending.

Collaboration: If you are planning to collaborate, collaborate with wise people. Think carefully before trusting anyone. A good person will give their best to make the work best. But a bad person will make the research miserable and you would not get good output. It is good to work with team but this is a kind of decision to make wisely.

Strength in your presentation: When you present your research work, make it stronger. Use PowerPoint presentations and use more examples. Make your presentation good so that no one end up with confusions. Clear everyone's doubt. Never make an incomplete presentation. Work more on your presentation style.

Seek for advice: You do not have to be secretive about your work. Be open. Talk to a professor for their guide. It is always a good practice to seek help so that whenever you stuck with something or have doubt they will help you clear it. Also you can show them for evaluation as the research work ends. But be careful do not give all the details to someone you cannot trust for your work. They are lot of people in world who copy people's work to get fame. Be aware of such tricksters.

Take time: Research works are time consuming and focus oriented work. Take walks or some free time to rest your mind. Mental space is important.

LXII

Positive and Negative Effects of Money on Our Personality

In today's society money is directly proportional to respect. If you have money than people respect you but if you don't have money you are considered a low class in society. Money also creates a different image of an individual in other's mind. Sometimes two people from which one is rich, and the other is poor do the same thing, the one who is poor will be considered to be the bad one or the one causing a negative impact.

For example, consider two men one rich and other one poor shopping, if both people made a mistake of forgetting to pay bill for a certain item then there will be two different results for the same mistake, in case of rich men it will be considered as an honest mistake but in case of the poor men there will be a very high chance that he will be considered a thief. This is just the belief of the society but there are many effects of money on an individual too like by gaining more money some people can become arrogant, and many other changes are also observed.

There are two different things here. One is getting money like winning a lottery or just doing a little thing to get money, and another is getting rich which involves a process of hard work and commitment in both the cases personality change but differently. Usually getting rich which involves hard work has a positive impact on your personality because you did many things to gain money, but when you get the money, it can have a negative impact on one's personality. Moreover, the effects are money is more on cognitive functioning than the personality which means money has a bigger impact on the thinking process rather than personality. Like when you become rich the value of money will decrease in your life because you have loads of it. You can buy whatever you need or whatever you like and don't care about the other necessary bills. But you will forget that other people don't have lots of money and they still value money because they have to take care of the basic bills like monthly rent, groceries, etc.

When getting the money, they start to think of everything has a price and you can buy it. They don't acknowledge the reality of money. They don't have to care about health plans like the working class people because they don't know the suffering of people with less money. The struggles of not having a health plan. Whenever they are sick, they can turn to the best medical facility because they have money.

Most of the people with more money are arrogant. Instead of controlling the money they let money control their lives. They think that they are above all just because they have more money. They can't step on the ground, and they always think highly of themselves.

Money also brings conflict in relationships. Some people will pretend to be good to them only because they have lots of money. They don't respect them truly. The people with more money judge the ones with less money as vice versa. The people with less money thinks that rich people become arrogant after getting the money and because of that they don't meet the people with less money. But in reality, rich people might be busy because they have more responsibilities too. They need to keep doing work to be rich, so they don't have time to meet everyone which make the people with less money think of them as arrogant. But there is one positive effect here, you can learn to handle criticism very well, but you need to work for it. There are arrogant rich people also, but there are many who handle the criticism very well and are humble.

A very good positive effect of money is that they can start giving money to poor and charity to make the society better. They want to spread happiness to everyone with their money instead of taking pride in money and letting the money control your life. So we can say money can also bring the quality of compassion and sharing in an individual.

The people who get money by doing little usually rationalize themselves by thinking that they truly deserve it. This is a negative impact of money on personality. It let us believe in false success. In reality, you didn't do much, but you have money, so you are successful.

People with more money tend to ignore pedestrians. This is again where they tend to think of themselves as the greatest and ignore others. There is a study conducted on this which revealed that people with expensive cars are more likely not to stop for the pedestrians to cross the road. This also means that they are also the ones who are more likely to break the law because getting away from the law can also be achieved by money. So one more negative effect due to money is the less fear of the law.

Another study revealed that people with less money are better at reading the facial expression. This is mainly because the problem faced by poor people are more and they know the effect of the problem in one's face hence they can read facial expressions easily. While on the other hand, the rich people spent their whole life in luxury and unaware of the daily life problems like hunger and financial distress. Therefore, they are incapable of recognizing what a person's face is indicating because they have never encountered such situations and have no knowledge about it.

Money has its impact on one's life, but the main problem is the individual. It's his/her choice to let the money drive them. In today's world, there are fewer people with more money and a big heart. Most of them are arrogant and think of themselves as the greatest. If all of them will have a big heart, then the money crisis in the whole world can be solved easily. But when this happens, the rich won't have an unfair advantage in the world that's why they are not willing to do such a thing because who doesn't want an unfair advantage over others.

"Don't limit yourself. Many people limit themselves to what they think they can do." – Mary Kay Ash

LXIII

Strategies For Professional Growth And Successful Career

Having a successful career comes with a lot of benefits and real profitable opportunities. As our society is governed by status and money, working your way up to the top improves your quality of life. A successful career offers you a feeling of security and accomplishment and to achieve it a gradual growth in professional life is essential. Abiding by certain practices and habits has benefitted a large number of successful individuals around the world. Here are some of those useful practices listed below:

Strategies for Successful Career

1. Identify with Your Goals

Before aiming to be successful in a career, identify yourself and the career path that suits you. Know your innermost desires. Think about the goals you want to achieve and evaluate whether they are in synchronization with your desires. To have a successful career, your desires and goals must coincide.

2. Build a Professional Resume

A resume is basically a list of your capabilities and previous experiences. A neat and impressive resume is pivotal to gain the attention of your employers and consequently build a successful career. Opportunities are everywhere, and to grab those you should be ready with a perfect or impressive resume preferably designed by professionals.

3. Become Aware of Your Strengths

Self-awareness is an essential key to the development of a successful career. By being aware of your inner thoughts, strengths, desires, advantages, and disadvantages, you can adapt yourself to any situation. You will also get the leverage of choosing a career best suited to your traits and qualities and will thus be successful in it.

4. Assume Full Responsibility for Your Life

Start assuming responsibility for your actions and do not blame anyone for your mistakes. To be successful in your career, do not take things personally, and whenever something bad happens, you need to assume it. Even if you are not directly connected to the mishap, your previous actions and thoughts might have caused it.

5. Always Raise Your Standards

Your standards influence your thoughts and behavior. If your standards are high, you will always aim higher and progress further to have a successful career. People with high standards are mostly more successful than average people. Try to improve yourself bit by bit up until you've become the best version of yourself.

6. Brand Yourself

Branding is a very important factor nowadays. Big companies spend millions on improving their brand or image in the market. Professional employees should brand their names and services to improve them. Starting a blog, creating a professional social media profile, or simply providing good services is an effective way to create your own brand and be successful in your respective career.

7. Network

Networking helps to create opportunities and connections. When you meet new people, you get a chance to utilize their skills to your advantage. Creating profiles on LinkedIn, Twitter, and Facebook can help to build a successful career.

Essential Professional Growth Strategies

1. Being hardworking and persistent

Hard work and persistence are indispensable for professional growth and success. When you give in your best in every project, your work performance enhances. Your effort and dedication will be most certainly noticed and will boost your career.

2. Setting achievable professional growth goals

Before advancing for any project, think about your specialties and the kind of projects you want to work on. Once you have a big picture, set small goals. That way, you will easily achieve small objectives and be motivated to persist till the end.

3. Knowing your strengths and weaknesses

One of the important strategies for professional growth is to be aware of your strengths and weaknesses. Evaluate your strong areas and take up only those projects that utilize your capabilities but do not exploit your weaknesses.

4. Developing leadership skills

Leadership is not a position but a process. Developing leadership skills opens up greater opportunities in the professional environment for you. Thinking outside the box, working on your communication skills and improving emotional intelligence are effective ways to develop leadership skills.

5. Following your principles

To have a truly fulfilling career adhere to your beliefs regarding task management, business communication, and work-life balance. When your principles align with your work ethics and environment, you can be satisfied with your job.

6. Striving for excellence

Striving for excellence ensures that you deliver quality work that meets the standards. This involves determining the areas in your work that are good and can be enhanced as the next step.

7. Being able to handle criticism

One of the prerequisites for professional growth is the ability to handle criticism. Negative feedback not only increases your resilience in the workplace but also helps to identify those areas where you are not putting your best. Taking criticism in good stride ultimately enhances your range of abilities.

8. Tracking your progress

Working for betterment is of no use unless you can track your progress. No matter what task you do, map your progress after every week. This will show how much further you've gone to achieve your target and the shortcomings that prevent you from going further.

LXIV
Journaling

As teenagers, we all had a diary under our pillows or mattress. It was our escape because we wrote everything in that diary without feeling guilt or having the fear of getting judged by others. That diary contained everything that one could feel at a time. Every time you decided to write your feelings and emotions down on a piece of paper, you might have felt your head becoming lighter and your mind becoming clearer. But as we grew up the habit of maintaining a diary also faded. Journaling as an adult also has similar effects on your mind. Even though most people believe the art of journaling to be a waste of time in these fast-paced lives, it is noted that people with a journal have their feelings more under control compared to those who don't.

What is journaling?

You might have had heard about journaling quite often around you and in case you have always wondered what it meant, then don't worry we have got you covered. In simple English terms, journaling is the process of writing your feelings and emotions down on a notebook regularly to help yourself understand them better. It is believed that every time you decide to write your emotions and feelings, you project them in a more organized way which helps you to keep your mind organized and focused.

People struggling with anxiety, depression, or even stress are always recommended to journal their feelings regularly to gain more control of their emotions and thus improve their mental health slowly.

What are the benefits of journaling regularly?

If you happen to be someone who gets overwhelmed easily then journaling is your solution to have your emotions in check. Regular journaling helps you to understand your feelings well as well it is a healthier way of expressing them instead of lashing out at people or even breaking down in front of people. It is one of the most efficient tools which can act as a helping hand to improve your mental health. Studies have shown that regular journaling is known to manage severe anxiety of different kinds, reduce work stress or emotional stress and even positively cope with depression.

How does journaling reduce and manage symptoms of psychological disorders?

In case you are wondering how regular journaling helps you to manage your psychological disorders then it reduces the symptoms and improves your mood slowly due to a lot of reasons. It allows you to focus on your emotions, problems, fears, and even concerns. Right from organizing them in a better manner to even helping you in identifying them and even prioritizing them in order. If you are someone who suffers from psychological disorders for a prolonged time, then you must note down the symptoms and signs that you experience regularly. It will help you identify any change or improvement in your mental state of being.

When you are suffering from mental disorders, even the slightest improvement is worth appreciation. Journaling is also a way of allowing yourself to engage in positive self-talk along with helping you to identify your toxic traits and negative behavior patterns. If you suffer from prolonged stress, then maintaining a journal will help you to identify what is the root cause of the stress so that you can then focus on finding the solution that will reduce stress. The key is to find the root cause or even causes which is causing stress so that you can work on resolving the problems and thus reduce the stress effectively.

Things to note in a journal regularly

To help manage your stress, anxiety, or even your depression better, start writing down your eating habits, whether you meditated or not, and even the amount of time you took for exercising. In addition to that, you also need to mention the number of hours you slept at night, and last but not the least, you proceed down to writing about your feelings and emotions that you experienced throughout the day. Make the language easy and simple for you to understand, there should be no attempt of pretending when you are journaling. You can even draw at times when you feel like you aren't able to put words to your feelings. The key is to focus on journaling regularly, you must turn journal writing into a habit.

Tip to maintain a journal regularly

Here's an effective tip that has helped numerous people in making journaling a habit, take 10-15 minutes out before going to bed at night for writing your journal. You can write everything you experienced during the day including your activities and call it a night. Keeping a journal is an escape every time you feel like your mind is a chaos and the world around you is loud and noisy.

LXV
Time Management For High Performers

Like Aristotle said, "Excellence is a habit, not an act" time management should also become a habit, an everyday practice. For those of you who are wondering what practice is, then it is the process of repeatedly acting regularly. Our lives currently are very fast-paced and there is hardly any time to rest or even sleep. We are connected to the world through social media apps and different time zones are hardly a factor. This is one of the main reasons why when we sit on mother nature's lap every once in a while and turn off our smartphones, the world around us seems to have a calming and soothing effect on us.

Even though we are not suggesting you toss your smartphone out in the bin, we are suggesting a couple of rules following which you will be able to manage your time better and provide high performance. Even though most people believe that to better manage their time and become high performers, they need to fall completely off the grid. However, not only that is impossible but also not realistic and rational. Certain behavioral changes and lifestyle changes can result in better time management thus making you a high performer. Don't believe us? Continue reading till the very end because we are mentioning little changes which you could include in your daily life.

Stop checking your phone the moment you wake

It has been noted that people check their phones even before they wake up properly in the morning. High performers don't engage themselves in checking social media apps the moment they wake up. It is a very unhealthy habit of checking your smartphones even before you touch your feet on the floor. Studies show that high performers go to bed with a plan regarding their activities for the next day. High performers are known to mind their own business at the break of dawn and throughout most of the day.

Schedule your telephonic conversations

Always make sure to engage yourself in scheduled conversations over the phone only. The moment you do otherwise, your current engagement is disrupted and you are distracted. It is always advised to take up unscheduled calls especially if we are engaged in high-value work. If you practice not receiving unscheduled calls regularly then you will note how your schedule is making clearer and your priorities are not changing.

Schedule time for you to go through your emails

Checking emails is an activity that if not set timing could take up the whole day. It is always advised to set a pre-determined time 2-3 times throughout the day so that you can go through your emails with ease. If you are required to instant reply to the incoming emails, then you could set a generic automated email reply on your email account. Prefer the 3D's rule when going through emails, either you deal with it, delegate with it or delete the emails.

Limit the distractions

Every time you are about to engage yourself in a work, try to keep your phone away so that you do not have the urge to check it every time there is a notification popping up on the screen. It will not only the work but also prevent you from focusing on the work at hand. The latter might lead to distractions and delays. Multitasking is efficient only when you are talking about two or more tasks at hand and not a smartphone in the equations.

Make a plan and make it a point to stick to it

Effective time management includes a lot of healthy practices regularly and there are no accidents that could lead to better time management. It requires extensive planning and strategizing your priorities for the next day, every day before you go to bed at night. It requires you to be strict with yourself so that you get to stick by the schedule which you have created for yourself.

The key is to be adamant and stick to the plan so that your time is managed according to the plan. In addition to that, sticking to a plan will also ensure that you are not getting yourself involved in any last-minute distractions.

Conclusion- time management and high performance

Now that you are aware of how time management and high performance are proportional to each other, you need to work on the former to provide the latter. If you are not good at managing time regularly then you wouldn't be able to provide optimum performance both on a personal and professional front. Therefore, you need to plan a schedule, avoid unnecessary screen time and maintain proper eating and sleeping habits. Little changes in the behaviors and lifestyles of people could go a long way and help them to better manage their time and become high performers with consistent efforts.

LXVI
Who is a Failure and How He/She Will Win Again?

Failure is the state where you do not get what you intend for. A failure is not a person; it is the state of mind. If you accept your faith as failure, you will end up being a failure. If you fight to stand as a successful person and take vow to fight with failure you can achieve victory. First we will discuss what is winning? In sports or competition, the meaning of winning is clear. Defeating others and getting prize. But what is winning when we talk about life.

Winning in life deals with weather we are learning, growing and succeeding. The meaning of winning according to Merriam-Webster is: "to get possession of by effort or fortune; to obtain by work: earn". The lovely words describe is winning is to obtain by work, to earn. No person can win all the time. There are ups and downs. If you are failing that means you are going to touch the success the next minute. Winning and failing are relative to each other. Failure does not mean it is the end, it means the new start.

From our childhood we learn about failure as we learn to race or participate in competitions. So if we are not able to fulfil something or get something we take it as our loss. This kind of thinking is planted on our minds from childhood. It is not your mistake to get disappointed; it is that planted part telling you that you are a loser. But in reality you are never a loser. There is so much to live for in life, a small disappointment does not make you a failure. As people we recognise other people's success and admire it, but we never take deep look into the struggle they have gone through to reach that height of success. We only compare ourselves with their success that is unfortunate for today's generation.

We often fail to find our errors and to correct them. We are so busy comparing ourselves with someone else's life. The world is now scared of failure and that leads to not even starting to do something new. If we take examples; award winning author J.K. Rowling who is famous worldwide for "Harry Potter" bosoms failure: "It is impossible to live without failing at something, unless you live so cautiously that you might as well not have lived at all-in which case, you fail by default". She herself has faced failures but she never stopped which now everyone can witness. But the question is how can we overcome the failure? How can we train our minds to accept the failure and not to stop?

Here are few steps to help you take a positive turn in your life:

Accept the failure: In our tough times, people tell us to "be positive". This feels frustrating as we have misconception about the word "positive". Being positive is not being happy or smiling. Positive thinking is learning and growing. Whenever you face failure, accept it. Try to learn something from your mistakes and grow yourself. Whenever you fail, accept that it is not the final destination. Always remember the best is yet to come. The failure was just a step towards success. So to overcome failure, learn to accept it first. It is okay to be upset or get disappointed for the failure but your goal is to not stop.

Let your frustration out: To let go something, all you need is to clear your mind. Initially you will feel emotional rush, you will feel frustrated and that is normal. Let it out. Then you will slowly return to your goal and you will be able to focus 100%.

Be Honest: The most difficult part of this process is to take some time to analyse the failure. You should take time to think what has happened and reason of what happened. Be honest about it. Most of the people do not do it. People are afraid to take blame on themselves. People are afraid to be honest with them, to take the guilt of the mistakes they have committed. But this is the important part where we need to improve. If we do not analyze the failure, we would never know the part where we had gone wrong. No matter how difficult it is, take the responsibility of your mistakes. Albert Einstein said "it is insane to do the same thing over and over again and expect a different result". We have to learn from our mistakes to overcome it. If not they we will be repeating our mistakes again and again and never be able to progress.

Fail Forward: We fail and go forward by learning from our mistakes and by making corrections to our errors until we get success. Every people we come across, every modification we make and every bit of data we soak up come together to produce a different outcome. We can't stop from something wrong to happen or some obstacle to come on our path but we have the power to handle them. Though we get panicked or stop thinking what to do for sometime but as we take time to think about it, we discover many ways to achieve our goal. It is all matter of time. As we take time to analyze, we discover new ways waiting for us which we have never thought of. As we become efficient handler, we are able to see the positive side of everything.

Failure is very true but it is never the end. Experiencing failure does not make you a failure but accepting the failure and stepping back does. You should accept the failure to go forward. A person, who has failed a lot, has experienced many risks and is unlikely to commit more mistakes than other. Failure is a chance to learn. Use this opportunity to become successful. Always struggle to find flaws from your processes and try not to repeat it. You will be repeatedly commit same mistakes if you do not learn from your mistakes.

LXVII
Most Successful Self-Help Blogs

A blog can be defined as web page or websites which uploads some contents with keeping the regular frequency, the content can be something to anything, but the wordings and the writing style is unconventional and conversational. In today's time, many individuals see this as an opportunity to showcase the talent inside them and is this the best way for the public reaches.

One can find anything here as there are many writers out there on every topic. But currently many individuals find it difficult to reach out for the best one out there as per their liking as they can find easily about the common kinds of stuff like technology or foods or travel but the real deal here is about self-help, and sometimes these blogs really provide viewer tips and tricks to attain the way towards self-help. So below here is the list of most successful self-help blogs of 2019-

- Addicted two success- This is a life design blog which was founded by Joel brown in 2011, and then he started sharing self-development stories to the worldwide audience. Apart from reading the content, the viewer can also have access to some motivational audio and video of some motivational leaders. This blog has eight posts per week frequency with around 837k Facebook followers and 663k twitter followers. Blog link- addicted2success.com

- Zen habits- This blog comes under the category of Mindfulness and happiness blog. Created in 2016 by Davis with a frequency of around two posts per week and this makes this tending in 2019. This blog is all about finding simplicity and happiness in daily life problems. This also gives the idea to the viewers about how to remove the extra workload and be free by creating something amazing out of nothing. This has twitter followers around 190K. Blog link- zenhabits.net

- Marc and angel hack life- From articles on the topics of personal development to social skills this blog has it all. With a frequency of one quality article per week this blog also helps the variety of readers by providing articles on the topic of life hacks, wealth, tech tricks and happiness. This is like a rainbow with the best intensity of all colors. This blog has around 273k followers on Facebook and around 57k followers on twitter. Blog link- marcandangel.com

• 4-Hour work week- Time Ferriss is the creator of this blog which is specialized in dealing with lifestyle problems and the workplace problem. This also helps the readers to break the chain of that 9-5 job routines and inspires them with some daily life examples, and it also provides them proper guidance. With the frequency of the posts being a single post per week this has around 41k facebook followers and 1.4 million Twitter followers. Blog link- fourhourworkweek.com/blog

• Marie forleo- This blog is famous among the readers with its unique style of conveying the information to the audience in a stylistic way like video with high quality and content. Apart from this blog also inspires the individual to live their dream and live freely. The creator of this blog is Marie whom herself is very motivated and uplifted being. This blog has a frequency of 2 posts per month as quality comes with a price, but this doesn't let the readers for wanting more. Its facebook followers are around 500k, and the twitter followers are around 194k. Blog link- marieforleo.com/blog

• Jack Canfield- This blog is like a more professional one which deals with personal development and creating a path for individuals success. This briefs the readers the ways and tips on how to achieve these things by showing them real-life examples. This blog was developed by Jack Canfield with a frequency of 3 posts per month with quality assured. This bog has around 1 million Facebook followers, and its Twitter followers are around 1.1 million. Blog link- jackcanfield.com/blog

• Finer minds- If one is searching something which should be related to learning new things, personal development of the individuals, growth in the business, enlightened ideas or something inspirational, then this is the right blog to visit. Its frequency is six posts per week which means one post per day. The Facebook followers of this blog are around 614k, and the twitter followers are around 13k. Blog link- finerminds.com

• The happiness project- The creator of this blog is Gretchen Rubin who is also the author of several record-breaking books; one of them is the famous "The happiness project." Hera at this blog she tells about the different and new methods of adopting and finding happiness in the day to day life schedules. This blog has two posts per week frequency with its Facebook followers amounting to 250k, and the twitter followers are around 134k. Blog link- gretchenrubin.com.

Success magazine- This blog is for the readers who are willing to take full responsibility for their doings. This blog understands that this world is changing so people should also change with it and this blog also provides some tips on that. Its frequency is one post per day with its Facebook followers being around 3.6 million and the twitter followers are around 315k.

LXVIII

SWOT Analysis

SWOT analysis is a technique that helps a person or organization to strategically plan and identify the strengths, weaknesses, opportunities, and threats that affect their business. This helps to clarify the objectives and identify the internal and external factors that boosters them.

SWOT is an acronym for the following four parameters:

Strengths: aspects of the business that favors it.

Weaknesses: characteristics of the business that are at a disadvantage.

Opportunities: elements that can be exploited to advantage in business.

Threats: elements that can harm a business or project.

Strategic fit highlights the degree to which the internal and external environment of a firm are compatible. SWOT analysis is important because they can throw light on future planning steps that will help achieve the objective. Decision makers should study the SWOTs and examine whether a target is attainable or not. If the objective is not attainable, they must opt for a different objective and repeat the process.

Internal Factors

SWOT analysis aims to identify the primary internal and external factors required to achieve an objective. SWOT analysis groups the information into two main categories:

Internal factors — the strengths and weaknesses of an organization

External factors — the opportunities and threats presented by the external environment to the organization

The analysis may classify strengths and weaknesses according to the different objectives of an organization. What acts as strengths concerning one objective may pose as a weakness for another objective.

External Factors

The external factors include:

Macroeconomic matters

Technological change

Legislation

Sociocultural changes

Changes in the marketplace.

The result is presented in the form of a matrix.

SWOT analysis is just a basic method of categorization and has its disadvantages. For example, it tends to persuade its users to prepare lists rather than to analyze the real important factors pivotal in achieving objectives. It uncritically presents the resulting lists, and without clearly prioritizing them, for example, weak opportunities may appear to be balancing active threats. It is wise not to eliminate any candidate using SWOT entry too quickly. The importance of individual SWOT analysis reveals the value of strategies generated by it.

How to Do a SWOT Analysis

Determine the objective: Decide on the key idea of the project or strategy that is to be analyzed and place it on the top of the page.

Create a grid: Draw a large square and divide it into four equally small squares.

Label each box: Write the word Strength inside the top left the box, Weaknesses inside the top right box, Opportunities inside the bottom left the box and Threats inside the bottom right box. These titles should be distinguished from one another by the use of varying text concerning both font color and font size. Smart Draw offers various SWOT diagram templates for this purpose.

Add strengths and weaknesses: Jot down the factors that affect the project in the respective boxes. Components of a SWOT analysis can be qualitative, anecdotal, quantitative, or empirical. Factors are generally listed in a bullet or numbered form.

Conclude: Analyze the finished SWOT diagram. Make sure that the positive outcomes do not outweigh the negative. If they do, it may not be a good decision to carry out the objective. Make adjustments accordingly or else simply abandon the plan.

Tips for a Successful SWOT analysis

Before conducting a SWOT analysis, decide what you want to achieve with it and consider whether it is aptly suited for your needs. If you decide a SWOT analysis is the best tool, the following tips will help you to analyze it better:

Keep your SWOT short and simple, but do not forget to include the important details.

When you finish your SWOT analysis, prioritize the results by listing them in descending order of the most significant factors to the least significant factors that affect your business.

Get multiple opinions and perspectives on your business for your SWOT analysis. Ask for input from the people involved in the business of those who help to run it, for example, employees, suppliers, customers, and partners.

Apply your SWOT analysis to a particular issue, such as a target you need to reach or a problem that requires a solution, rather than to the entire business. You can then conduct separate SWOT analyses and combine their results to get an overall output.

Look at where your business is now and think about the amount of growth you want to envisage in the future.

Consider your competitors' share in the market and realistically compare how much your business competes with them.

Think about the factors that are essential to the growth of your business, and the things only you or your business can offer to the market and customers, but your competitors cannot. This is called a competitive advantage, and it can be a turning point in the SWOT analysis.

Utilize the objective of the overall business or project in your SWOT analysis.

100 Questions Needed To Be Asked About Life

What is the meaning of life?

The meaning of life varies for each individual, but it often involves finding purpose, happiness, and fulfillment.

How can I find my purpose in life?

Finding your purpose involves exploring your passions, values, and interests. It may require self reflection, trying new things, and following your intuition.

What is the key to happiness?

Happiness is subjective, but it often stems from having meaningful relationships, pursuing personal growth, and finding gratitude in life's small pleasures.

How can I overcome fear?

Overcoming fear can be achieved through facing your fears, building self-confidence, and reframing negative thoughts.

What is the importance of self-care?

Self-care is essential for maintaining physical, mental, and emotional we l-being. It involves prioritizing activities that replenish and rejuvenate you.

How can I achieve a work-life balance?

Achieving work-life balance requires setting boundaries, prioritizing self-care, and effectively managing time and energy.

How do I cope with stress?

Coping with stress involves adopting healthy coping mechanisms such as exercise, mindfulness, seeking support, and practicing relaxation techniques.

What is the role of gratitude in life?

Practicing gratitude can enhance well-being by shifting focus to the positive aspects of life and fostering a sense of contentment and appreciation.

How do I build resilience?

Building resilience involves developing a positive mindset, cultivating strong social connections, and actively seeking personal growth through challenging experiences.

How can I improve my communication skills?

Improving communication skills can be achieved through active listening, empathy, clarity, and practicing effective verbal and non-verbal communication techniques.

What is the importance of setting goals?

Setting goals provides direction, motivation, and a sense of purpose. It helps you prioritize and work towards achieving your dreams and aspirations.

How can I build healthy relationships?

Building healthy relationships involves effective communication, trust, respect, and mutual support. It requires open-mindedness, empathy, and a willingness to compromise.

How can I manage my time effectively? Managing time effectively involves setting priorities, creating a schedule, avoiding procrastination, and learning to say no when necessary.

What is the role of failure in life? Failure is a natural part of life and can be a valuable learning experience. It helps build resilience, provides opportunities for growth, and teaches important lessons.

How can I develop a positive mindset?

Developing a positive mindset involves practicing gratitude, reframing negative thoughts, surrounding yourself with positive influences, and focusing on personal growth.

What is the secret to success?

Success is subjective, but it often involves setting goals, working hard, persevering through challenges, and continuously learning and adapting.

How can I find motivation?

Finding motivation involves aligning your goals with your values, breaking tasks into manageable steps, seeking inspiration, and celebrating small victories.

How can I make a positive impact on the world?

Making a positive impact on the world can be achieved through acts of kindness, volunteering, advocating for important causes, and being mindful of your environmental footprint.

How do I deal with failure?

Dealing with failure involves embracing it as an opportunity for growth, learning from mistakes, and maintaining a resilient mindset. It's important to not let failure define you.

What is the key to a fulfilling career?

A fulfil ling career often involves finding work that aligns with your passions, values, and strengths. It's about finding a sense of purpose and personal satisfaction.

How can I cultivate self-discipline?

Cultivating self-discipline involves setting clear goals, creating routines, breaking tasks into smaller steps, and practicing consistency and perseverance.

How can I overcome procrastination?

Overcoming procrastination involves understanding the underlying causes, breaking tasks into smaller, manageable parts, setting deadlines, and creating a supportive environment.

What is the importance of self-reflection?

Self-reflection a lows you to gain insight into your thoughts, emotions, and behaviors. It helps you make better decisions, understand yourself better, and grow as an individual.

How do I let go of the past?

Letting go of the past involves accepting what you cannot change, forgiving yourself and others, focusing on the present, and seeking support if needed.

How can I manage my finances effectively?

Managing finances effectively involves creating a budget, tracking expenses, saving money, and making informed financial decisions.

What is the importance of lifelong learning?

Lifelong learning is essential for personal growth, adaptability, and staying intellectually engaged. It broadens knowledge, enhances ski ls, and opens doors to new opportunities.

How can I improve my problem-solving skills? Improving problem-solving ski ls involves analyzing situations, seeking alternative solutions, practicing critical thinking, and learning from past experiences.

How can I cultivate a healthy lifestyle?

Cultivating a healthy lifestyle involves adopting balanced eating habits, regular exercise, prioritizing sleep, managing stress, and avoiding harmful substances.

How can I improve my self-confidence?

Improving self-confidence involves cha lenging self limiting beliefs, setting achievable goals, celebrating achievements, and surrounding yourself with supportive people.

What is the importance of forgiveness?

Forgiveness is crucial for personal growth and mental well-being. It releases negative emotions, promotes healing, and a lows for the development of healthier relationships.

How can I overcome self-doubt?

Overcoming self-doubt involves challenging negative self-talk, focusing on strengths and achievements, seeking support, and practicing self compassion.

What is the secret to maintaining long-lasting friendships?

Maintaining long-lasting friendships requires trust, open communication, mutual respect, and investing time and effort in nurturing the relationship.

How can I manage conflict effectively?

Managing conflict effectively involves active listening, empathy, seeking common ground, and finding mutually beneficial solutions.

What is the importance of travel?

Travel broadens horizons, exposes you to different cultures and perspectives, fosters personal growth, and creates lasting memories.

How can I cultivate a positive body image?

Cultivating a positive body image involves focusing on self-acceptance, practicing self-care, challenging societal beauty standards, and surrounding yourself with positive influences.

How can I build emotional intelligence?

Building emotional intelligence involves developing self-awareness, empathy, effective communication skills, and learning to manage emotions in a healthy way.

What is the importance of hobbies and leisure activities?

Hobbies and leisure activities provide a sense of joy, relaxation, and personal fulfillment. They can reduce stress, boost creativity, and contribute to overall well-being.

How can I overcome social anxiety?

Overcoming social anxiety involves gradually exposing yourself to social situations, challenging negative thoughts, seeking support, and practicing relaxation techniques.

How can I develop effective leadership skills?

Developing effective leadership skills involves setting a positive example, inspiring others, communicating vision, and continuously learning and improving.

What is the importance of self-acceptance?

Self-acceptance is crucial for mental health and well-being. It involves embracing your strengths and weaknesses, accepting your imperfections, and practicing self-compassion.

How can I cultivate a positive work environment?

Cultivating a positive work environment involves fostering open communication, recognizing and appreciating employees, promoting work-life balance, and providing growth opportunities.

How can I build financial security?

Building financial security involves saving money, investing wisely, managing debt, and having a financial plan for the future.

What is the importance of empathy?

Empathy allows you to understand and share the feelings of others. It fosters compassion, strengthens relationships, and promotes a sense of connection and belonging.

How can I overcome burnout?

Overcoming burnout involves setting boundaries, practicing self-care, seeking support, and reassessing priorities to create a healthier work-life balance.

What is the importance of self-education?

Self-education allows you to pursue knowledge and skills outside of traditional educational institutions. It empowers you to take control of your learning journey and explore your interests.

How can I cultivate a positive mindset in challenging times?

Cultivating a positive mindset in challenging times involves focusing on gratitude, seeking support, practicing resilience, and maintaining hope.

How can I build effective teamwork skills?

Building and fostering effective teamwork skills involves open communication, promoting collaboration, valuing diverse perspectives, and recognizing individual strengths.

What is the importance of boundaries in relationships? B

Boundaries in relationships are essential for maintaining healthy dynamics. They define what is acceptable and help establish mutual respect, trust, and emotional well-being.

How can I overcome imposter syndrome?

Overcoming imposter syndrome involves recognizing your achievements, reframing negative thoughts, seeking support, and embracing self-compassion.

What is the importance of creativity in life?

Creativity allow for self-expression, problem-solving, and innovation. It enhances personal fulfillment, boosts mental well-being, and contributes to a more vibrant world.

How can I improve my public speaking skills?

Improving public speaking skills involves practice, preparation, effective storytelling, body language awareness, and connecting with the audience.

What is the importance of adaptability?

Adaptability is crucial for navigating change, embracing new opportunities, and thriving in dynamic environments. It allows for personal growth and resilience.

How can I develop effective decision-making skills?

Developing effective decision-making skills involves gathering information, weighing pros and cons, considering long-term consequences, and trusting your intuition.

How can I develop a growth mindset?

Developing a growth mindset involves embracing challenges, seeing failures as learning opportunities, seeking feedback, and believing in your ability to grow and improve.

What is the importance of self-compassion?

Self-compassion involves treating yourself with kindness and understanding, especially in times of difficulty or failure. It promotes resilience, well-being, and self-acceptance.

How can I cultivate patience?

Cultivating patience involves practicing mindfulness, reframing expectations, embracing uncertainty, and focusing on the present moment.

What is the importance of gratitude in relationships?

Expressing gratitude in relationships fosters appreciation, strengthens emotional bonds, and enhances overall relationship satisfaction.

How can I overcome loneliness?

Overcoming loneliness involves seeking social connections, joining groups or communities with shared interests, fostering self-compassion, and seeking professional help if needed.

How can I develop effective problem-solving skills?

Developing effective problem-solving skills involves breaking down problems into smaller parts, considering multiple perspectives, brainstorming creative solutions, and learning from past experiences.

What is the importance of self-compassion in times of failure?

Self-compassion in times of failure allows for self-acceptance, learning from mistakes, and maintaining emotional well-being. It helps you bounce back and grow from setbacks.

How can I build trust in relationships?

Building trust in relationships involves being reliable, honest, and consistent in your actions. It requires open communication, vulnerability, and respecting boundaries.

How can I cultivate a positive mindset in the face of adversity?

Cultivating a positive mindset in the face of adversity involves reframing challenges as opportunities, focusing on strengths, seeking support, and maintaining hope.

What is the importance of self-motivation?

Self-motivation drives you to take action, set and achieve goals, and persevere through challenges. It allows for personal growth and accomplishment.

How can I develop effective listening skills? Developing effective listening skills involves giving full attention, avoiding interruptions, asking clarifying questions, and practicing empathy.

How can I overcome negative self-talk?

Overcoming negative self-talk involves challenging irrational thoughts, reframing negative beliefs, and practicing self-compassion and self-acceptance.

What is the importance of self-awareness?

Self-awareness allows you to understand your emotions, thoughts, and behaviors. It promotes personal growth, authenticity, and better decision-making.

How can I build trust in myself?

Building trust in yourself involves setting realistic goals, following through on commitments, celebrating achievements, and learning from mistakes.

How can I embrace change?

Embracing change involves reframing it as an opportunity for growth, being open to new experiences, and practicing adaptability and resilience.

How can I build resilience in difficult times?

Building resilience in difficult times involves seeking support, maintaining a positive mindset, practicing self-care, and learning from challenging experiences.

What is the importance of personal values?

Personal values guide your actions, decisions, and priorities. They provide a sense of purpose, and authenticity, and help shape your identity.

How can I practice mindfulness?

Practicing mindfulness involves focusing on the present moment, cultivating awareness, and non-judgmental observing thoughts and sensations.

How can I build effective problem-solving skills in a team setting?

Building effective problem-solving skills in a team setting involves fostering open communication, encouraging diverse perspectives, collaboratively brainstorming solutions.

What is the importance of self-expression?

Self-expression allows you to communicate your thoughts, emotions, and creativity. It fosters authenticity, enhances well-being, and strengthens relationships.

How can I develop effective time management skills?

Developing effective time management skills involves setting goals, prioritizing tasks, creating a schedule, and avoiding procrastination.

How can I cultivate a positive mindset in the face of failure?

Cultivating a positive mindset in the face of failure involves reframing failure as an opportunity for growth, learning from mistakes, and practicing self-compassion.

What is the importance of self-motivation in achieving goals?

Self-motivation drives you to take action, persevere through challenges, and stay committed to achieving your goals. It fuels determination and resilience.

How can I build effective negotiation skills?

Building effective negotiation skills involves active listening, understanding perspective, the other party's seeking win-win solutions and maintaining assertiveness.

How can I develop effective study habits?

Developing effective study habits involves creating a conducive environment, setting clear goals, breaking down tasks, and using effective learning strategies.

What is the importance of self-acceptance in relationships?

Self-acceptance in relationships allows for vulnerability, authenticity, and healthy boundaries. It promotes acceptance of oneself and others.

How can I cultivate gratitude in daily life?

Cultivating gratitude in daily life involves keeping a gratitude journal, expressing appreciation to others, and regularly reflecting on the positive aspects of life.

How can I build effective problem-solving skills in the workplace?

Building effective problem-solving skills in the workplace involves analyzing problems, seeking input from colleagues, considering multiple perspectives, and implementing creative solutions.

What is the importance of self-reflection in decision-making?

Self-reflection in decision-making a lows you to align your decisions with your values, goals, and personal growth. It helps you make intentional choices.

How can I improve my self-awareness?

Improving self-awareness involves observing your thoughts, emotions, and behaviors, seeking feedback, and practicing self-reflection.

How can I cultivate a positive mindset in the face of rejection?

Cultivating a positive mindset in the face of rejection involves reframing rejection as redirection, focusing on strengths, seeking support, and maintaining self-belief.

What is the importance of social support?

Social support provides emotional, practical, and informational assistance during challenging times. It fosters a sense of belonging, resilience, and overall well-being.

How can I build effective problem-solving skills in personal relationships?

Building effective problem-solving skills in personal relationships involves active listening, empathy, seeking win-win solutions, and maintaining open communication.

How can I develop effective study skills?

Developing effective study skills involves creating a study schedule, using active learning techniques, minimizing distractions, and seeking clarification when needed.

What is the importance of self-care in relationships?

Self-care in relationships allows for personal well being, balance, and maintaining healthy boundaries. It promotes emotional resilience and contributes to relationship satisfaction.

How can I build effective conflict-resolution skills?

Building effective conflict resolution skills involves active listening, empathy, seeking common ground, and finding mutually beneficial solutions.

How can I cultivate a positive mindset in the face of criticism?

Cultivating a positive mindset in the face of criticism involves separating constructive feedback from personal attacks, focusing on growth opportunities, and practicing self-compassion.

What is the importance of self-compassion in relationships?

Self-compassion in relationships a lows for understanding, forgiveness, and acceptance of oneself and others. It promotes healthier dynamics and emotional well-being.

How can I build effective problem-solving skills in parenting?

Building effective problem-solving skills in parenting involves active listening, empathy, setting clear boundaries, and involving children in decision-making when appropriate.

How can I develop effective goal-setting skills?

Developing effective goal-setting skills involves setting specific, measurable, achievable, relevant, and time-bound (SMART) goals. It requires planning, tracking progress, and adapting as needed.

What is the importance of self-reflection in relationships?

Self-reflection in relationships allows for personal growth, understanding patterns, and recognizing areas for improvement. It contributes to healthier and more fulfilling connections.

How can I cultivate a positive mindset in the face of setbacks?

Cultivating a positive mindset in the face of setbacks involves reframing setbacks as opportunities for growth, focusing on solutions, seeking support, and maintaining resilience.

How can I build effective problem-solving skills in educational settings?

Building effective problem-solving skills in educational settings involves seeking help when needed, brainstorming alternative solutions, and actively participating in group discussions.

What is the importance of self-compassion in personal growth?

Self-compassion in personal growth a lows for self acceptance, learning from mistakes, and embracing growth opportunities.

It promotes resilience and well-being.

How can I cultivate a positive mindset in the face of uncertainty?

Cultivating a positive mindset in the face of uncertainty involves focusing on what you can control, embracing flexibility, seeking support, and maintaining optimism.

Best Of Luck.

10 Best affirmations For Being The G.o.a.t (greatest Of All Time):

1. "I am the best at what I do, and I keep improving every day."

2. "Success is in my DNA and welcomes me to my greatness with confidence."

3. "I get better and try harder when everyone needs me most because I thrive under pressure, and I turn challenges into victories."

4. "Every day, I outperform my past self and rise to new heights."

5. "My mindset is unshakeable and destined for legendary success."

6. "I push barriers, break limits, and inspire others."

7. "My skills are unmatched, and I continually hone them to perfection."

8. "I am a leader and greatness makes me remarkable as an example."

9. *"I welcome the road of becoming great and enjoy every step."*

10. "I am the one with the power, focus, and discipline to be the G.O.A.T in my field."

10 Meditation Practices That Can Help You To Be Greatest Of All Time (g.o.a.t.)

1. Visualization of Success:

- **Duration:** 10-15 minutes every day

- **Goal:** Build strength in your belief in your ultimate capacity.

- **Practice:** Close your eyes and imagine yourself being at the top of your game. Imagine everything-the sensation, the visual impressions, the audio, how other people respond to your success-all as clear as possible about emotion, pride, and satisfaction.

2. Affirmation Meditation:

- **Duration:** 5-10 minutes a day

- **Goal:** Build positive self-talk.

- **Practice:** Choose affirmations such as "I am the best at what I do," "I am strong," or "I make challenges turn into triumphs." Repeat them slowly in your mind, regulating your breathing in rhythm with your words.

3. Mindful Breathing to Focus:

- **Time:** Five minutes before focusing on activities that demand deep concentration

- **Goal:** Sharpen attention.

-**Practice:** Sit in a comfortable position with your eyes closed and focus on your breath. Count your breathing up to 10, then begin again. Whenever the thoughts recur, calmly bring your mind back to the breath. This is the basic physical preparation for mastery.

4. Body Scan for Physical Awareness:

-**Duration:** 10 minutes following intense exercise

- **Objective:** Develop body awareness and reduce tension.

- **Activity:** Lie down and then slowly bring your focus up the whole body, noticing where you're experiencing any tension. Inhale into each region and let go of the tension entirely. This is great for the athlete or the type of person who exercises strenuously.

5. **Gratitude Meditation:**

- **Duration:** 5-10 minutes per day

- **Focus:** Develop humility and temperance

- **Practice:** Reflect on the people, opportunities and skills that brought you to where you are today. Focus in a feeling of gratitude and let it fill you up. This may keep you grounded as you aim for excellence.

6. **Obstacle Reflection Meditation:**

- **Time:** 10 minutes a week

- **Focus:** Build resilience.

- **Practice:** Reflect on a recent obstacle or failure. Attend to your thoughts and emotions with neutral awareness. Visualize being able to overcome the challenge; pay attention to what you accomplished. This meditation can help in turning failures into milestones.

7. **Self-Compassion Meditation:**

- **Minutes per practice:** 5-10 minutes when you feel sad

- **What the meditation aims at achieving:** Reduces self-criticism and bounces back after failure.

- **Practice:** Sit with your eyes closed. Repeat, "May I be kind to myself," "May I accept myself just as I am," and "May I forgive myself for mistakes." Emphasize giving that same kindness you would give to a friend.

8. **Quiet Mind Meditation:**

- **Practice:** 15-20 minutes per day

- **Intentions:** Inspire creative thinking and clarity.

- **Practice:** Sit comfortably and just think without becoming attached to thoughts. Let each thought pass like a cloud. With practice, you will experience moments of silence and clarity, which can help turn on the lights of novel ideas and solutions.

9. Peak Performance Visualization:

- **Duration:** 10 minutes before major events-competitions, presentations, etc.

- **Goal:** To increase confidence and readiness.

Practice: You may do the visualization exercise. Imagine that you are at your best. Feel the energy, focus, and flow of the present moment. Imagine the result you would want to achieve: how it feels to gain it. Prime your mind for real-life performance.

10. Loving-Kindness Meditation:

Daily Time: 5-10 minutes

Goal: Building compassion and supportive community.

This includes practice: sending positive thoughts and good wishes to yourself, your loved ones, and even competitors. "May they be happy, may they be successful." It keeps those relationships healthy and balanced.

These meditations may prove useful in helping you build the mindset, resilience, and focus needed to be the GOAT in your chosen field. Start with a few that resonate most with your current needs, then expand as you build a habit of mindfulness.

Thank You

www.ingramcontent.com/pod-product-compliance
Lightning Source LLC
Chambersburg PA
CBHW070752160726
48004CB00001B/156